Complete Game

Complete Game

◆

The Emotional Dynamics of In-Game Focus

Rob Crews

iUniverse, Inc.
New York Lincoln Shanghai

Complete Game
The Emotional Dynamics of In-Game Focus

iUniverse books may be ordered through booksellers or by contacting:

iUniverse
2021 Pine Lake Road, Suite 100
Lincoln, NE 68512
www.iuniverse.com
1-800-Authors (1-800-288-4677)

Because of the dynamic nature of the Internet, any Web addresses or links contained in this book may have changed since publication and may no longer be valid.

The views expressed in this work are solely those of the author and do not necessarily reflect the views of the publisher, and the publisher hereby disclaims any responsibility for them.

ISBN: 978-0-595-43236-3 (pbk)
ISBN: 978-0-595-87577-1 (ebk)

Printed in the United States of America

Contents

Foreword. ix

Introduction xi

CHAPTER 1   The Three R's 1

CHAPTER 2   Hitters are Computers. 4

CHAPTER 3   N.E.O. Complex. 7

CHAPTER 4   Why You Can't Hit? Seven Reasons 9

CHAPTER 5   T.A.G. Talent, Ability, and Gifts. 11

CHAPTER 6   Make-Up and Muscle: Form and Power 14

CHAPTER 7   Making a Connection 16

CHAPTER 8   Re-Creating The Mindset 18

CHAPTER 9   Improving In-Game Focus 21

CHAPTER 10   Turning the Page. 24

CHAPTER 11   Multiple Chef Syndrome. 29

CHAPTER 12   Confidence is a Mindset?. 33

CHAPTER 13   CD's: Common Distractions. 38

CHAPTER 14   Focus Phases: The Game Face 45

CHAPTER 15   Change My Mind: Seasonal Mind-Sets (3
             Trimesters) 49

CHAPTER 16   It's The Thought that Counts 53

CHAPTER 17   Reconciliation: Body and Mind Synchronized. 57

CHAPTER 18   The Psycho Dad: the Passive Parent. 63

CHAPTER 19   Make it Happen: Goal Setting, Commitment, and
Time Management. 66

Athlete Goal Setting Worksheet. 69

Acknowledgements

I thank God for His involvement in the inspiration for this book. It is in Him that I move, in Him that I live, and in Him that I have my being. His Awesomeness humbles me and I am grateful.

Also, I thank my family for being understanding and granting me the space to complete such an awesome task. And finally, I would like to thank my students for teaching me so much. For the things revealed to me come as a result of the opportunity to help you.

Foreword

Teaching the great game of baseball and softball brings the master teacher to far away places. We start the journey with our students hoping that the road will be clear and the end results will be in reach. We begin with the teachings of the body and when the student is ready, we begin to teach the powers of the mind, the soul and the heart.

The master teacher inspires within each of his students the desire to learn and grow. The master teacher's most important task is one of teaching body and emotional awareness to the young student; to challenge the student to create the future within their mind's eye. The master teacher speaks the language of the emotions—by inspiring, motivating and encouraging love of the sport and love for life.

For years, I have seen the author grow from willing student to accomplished teacher. His life work and commitment to excellence clearly belies his chronological age. The lives he has touched transcend the dirt infields and peaceful outfield grass where he has applied his trade. I have seen Rob at the start of his journey and with admiration, now walk with him on the never-ending road to be the master teacher. In softball, baseball and in life, the teachings and wisdom within this book will inspire others to one day walk on the road of the master teacher.

—Tony Abbatine, National Director of Training, Frozen Ropes

Introduction

Frozen Ropes Training Center is where I received my formal training in how to teach the game. Under the tutelage of Tony Abbatine, the founder of the Frozen Ropes Training Centers and its concepts, I learned and have become very effective at training hitters for in-game success. The Complete Game concept was birthed out of the Frozen Ropes Teaching Model and organized into a system of synergizing or combining mind and body training.

For sake of this book, my aim is to heighten the awareness of players, coaches and parents to the mental, psychological, and emotional dynamics of in-game focus, which ultimately translates into on-field success. IN-GAME FOCUS and Distraction Management are one; they are synonymous. And Thought Management is the beginning of Distraction Management. Distractions cannot be managed until our thoughts are managed. If we can train our players to think on the good things and give less attention to the bad things, what a perfect world competition would be. The bottom line is that many players never fully understand this. They never understand that it is ALL GOOD. The good is good and the bad is even better. Usually the bad helps one to grow and get some adversity and experience under our belt. *Adversity* and *Experience* should be synonyms. The tough times we go through make future tough times a bit easier to handle. Adverse situations create an opportunity for us to overcome something.

> *"...whatever is true, whatever is noble, whatever is right, whatever is pure, whatever is lovely, whatever is admirable—if anything is excellent or praiseworthy—think about such things."*
> *-Philippians 4:8 NIV*

Complete Game was written in order to bring out what lies deep inside of many athletes who struggle with being able to perform at their Full Genetic Potential on a consistent basis. Your Genetic Potential is that inherited ability which comes from either your parents or their parents which also lies inside of you. Here is an example: Let's say I have three cups of coffee on the table. The green cup has a lot of sugar at the bottom, the yellow cup has a little bit, and the red cup has none. I can take a sip from each and they will all taste the same. The green cup will probably taste just a bit sweeter than the others, but not much. The only way I can get the yellow cup to taste sweet is if I stir up the sugar on the bottom. The red cup will never be sweet no matter how much I stir. Well, Complete Game is that spoon that stirs up what lies dormant or on the bottom of an athlete. If you can sense that there is something special about a player, but they are falling short, then you need a way to stir up what lies deep inside of them. However, if there is a player with no potential, then you cannot stir up what is not there. He is like the red cup. This book is written for Green and Yellow players. The best way to stir up that which is not on the surface is to change how we think, not how we act. For it is the way we think, that affects our responses. It is the thought process that determines our actions.

Answers.com defines ***the mind*** as: *n. 1. The human consciousness that originates in the brain and is manifested especially in thought, perception, emotion, will, memory, and imagination. 2. The collective conscious and unconscious processes in a sentient organism that direct and influence mental and physical behavior.*

At Complete Game, we often talk about S.W.A.G. 101 or SWAG Training. The bottom line is that without SWAG Training, many athletes would come into a session, never bringing what they have learned, out onto the field. They would crumble when the curtain goes up. That would not only be frustrating for the player and parent, but also the teacher. So we spend a significant amount of time incorporating our SWAG Training or Mental Skills training into the sessions. SWAG Training consists of improving in-game focus, concentration, relaxation, confidence, and attitude. I have taken the time in this book to crack the code on training players with the intent to prepare them for better in-game focus. I have gotten a bit tired of training great players to have beautiful swings, only to go out and fail. The biggest reason for the failure is not always their physical ability, nor is it poor swing mechanics. The biggest reason for failure is 100% emotional. Emotions always contribute to the lack of focus and the wrong mindset. The time for running from facing the Mental Game is over. If we don't face it now, we'll have to face it later. RAW TALENT can only take you but so far.

Frankly there are just way too many athletes whose physical skills have gotten them to the top but their minds can't keep them there. There are baseball players who will never get out of AA due to the inability to focus at the level necessary for Major League success. There are also athletes in college who should have been Division I, but aren't. There are also hitters batting 8th, and perhaps could be number 3. So what I have noticed is that what separates one athlete from another is not always the skill level; but it is the MENTAL

SKILLS or the lack thereof. It is the ability to manage our emotions, and not have our emotions manage us. The ability and the inability to perform consistently, is not only about skills and talent, but mostly about what you are thinking about or not thinking about.

Many coaches and athletes will say the game is 80% mental but never spend enough time developing this part of their game. Is it because we don't know how? Or do we love to ignore those things we aren't good at? In sports and competition, mind activity and physical activity occur at the same time. When it is time to perform, we cannot get caught up into whatever emotions are going to distract us from achieving our Full Genetic Potential. So if your mental game is not up to par, then your entire game is really incomplete.

Can thoughts really be controlled? Can emotions really be managed? Thoughts cannot be controlled, and neither can our emotions. But the manifestations of our emotions can be controlled. So we don't have to cry just because we are sad. We don't have to laugh, just because something is funny. You can cry or laugh later. I understand that this is not possible for everyone. That is why there are only a few athletes who are capable of attaining this ultimate level of focus. And as I think back to certain players that I have trained over the years, I realized that the one's with the better mental skills were more consistent. Do your emotions control you or do you control your emotions?

We now have more technology than we have ever had. Hitters can study video and even study pitcher's deliveries and tendencies. There are training bats, videos, fancy tees, special balls, analysis software, hypnosis, etc. Yet with all this knowledge, PEOPLE STILL CAN'T HIT! Coaches are still debating who knows the most about hitting and who is right and who is wrong. We are making all these changes in swing movements and yet hitters are still struggling. Here's one more: hitters are struggling with the same issues in the 21st century as they did in 1985. Coaches are teaching players how to have nice swings, but not how to hit. I am really concerned about where coaching or training is going right now. However, I am not out to convince everyone that I know more than the next guy. I probably do, but who cares. Who are we kidding? Everything that is out there, is a compilation of different things from different people. So we all learn from each other. I get nervous when I meet coaches who know it all and have no interest in receiving or sharing. To me, they are not qualified to develop hitters. They are all about themselves.

Whatever you are doing as a coach or player is fine. If you believe it is the truth, and you are having some success, you should continue to perfect your hitting model. I AM NOT OUT TO CHANGE YOUR SWING, JUST YOUR MIND. But whatever you are doing, be sure it enables to you to be fast and strong. If you are fast and strong it is so much easier to be on time. That's what it's all about: TIME to COLLISION. Hitters need to be on time. A hitter must have the ability to see/evaluate a pitch and determine where the ball will be at the estimated time of impact. Mis-management of emotions always causes mental clutter, which impedes the perfection of this process. Complete Game offers some strategies that can be incorporated into your training model to increase focus and concentration, improve confidence and enhance relaxation. These are all skills-mental skills that CAN be improved. COMPLETE GAME outlines ways in which coaches and players can better understand and implement an effective MENTAL GAME PLAN. The objective: to help players and coaches re-define the thought-processes involved with training and then transitioning it into perfect performance.

Although I have written this book primarily to the baseball and softball world, I believe other sports can certainly relate. I believe softball has evolved to the place where it has now become gospel to preach that the softball and baseball swing are one and the same. This makes room for a baseball guy like myself to actually share his knowledge to the softball world and it be accepted. Finally! We're here! So if you have an open mind, I would like you to invite you on a journey with me into what I call the *Emotional Dynamics* of In-Game Focus or the Complete Game. Believe it or not, there are Emotional Dynamics to this. The part of the game many people talk about, but few can articulate or teach effectively - THE MENTAL GAME: The EMOTIONAL GAME.

A wise man once said, *"A thing must be good in the beginning, good in the middle, and good at the end."* Thus there are three parts of a swing: the beginning, middle, and end. To some, this might be (1) the setup, (2) the load or negative move, and then (3) the actual swing and/or follow through. Are the beginning, middle, and end of a swing only the part that the physical body performs? Or is there something that precedes even that? The physical swing is what we who think we know about hitting debate and fuss about. Hey, we all would like to think we are right. And for a long time I thought I was right. We all believe in what we teach and we share it with such passion and conviction- and we should. But then I began to realize that I was teaching something different every year. What was true last year isn't necessarily true this year: My understanding of what was working for my students increased. And as a result, I am not teaching the same things to hitters presently that I did two years ago. And two years from now, I probably won't be teaching the same thing I am today. I am sure many of you coaches/teachers can relate to this. This is merely evolution of hitting theories. We are getting better. The game has come a long way.

So the question remains: exactly what is the beginning of the process involved in the swing? And what is the proper way to teach it? Not just on the level of the little leaguer, but on the level of the ELITE ATHLETE.

1

The Three R's

There are three phases of the hitter's mental process that I spend time developing. It is my intent to break down the process for hitters, in sequential order and with brief explanations upon which I intend to expound upon in further detail later in the book. Have you ever heard the premise, *"See it and Hit it?"* I have taken this a step further and would like to present to you what I call the three R's. Read, Reconcile, and Respond/React.

First, we have to READ it or see it. The READ is essential because seeing it is everything. Seeing it is the first step in the process and is what many hitters and coaches know very little about. In fact, there are now eye doctors out there who know very little about hitting but are working with hitters to improve visual skills. Anyway, I have found that seeing it is not always a function of how good your eyes are, but how good your focus and concentration skills are. Visual misinformation is the primary reason for bad hitting mechanics. The SEE IT part usually precedes the HIT IT part and the HIT IT part has a lot to do with how we SEE IT. Since we are not mind readers, we can't look at a hitter and really know what they see. Neither can we know HOW they are tracking the moving ball or what their search patterns are. This is the mechanics of their vision or better said, Visual Mechanics. Visual Mechanics are what I call *THE INVISIBLE WEAPON*. It is invisible, mainly because it cannot be seen. Visual Mechanics do not show up on video. We at Frozen Ropes have been teaching this concept for some time, while other *'batting cages'* focus on arguing over swing mechanics. The bottom line is you can be successful with a bad swing and great visual skills, but you can't be consistent with a perfect swing and poor visual skills. So we need both. Great swing mechanics and Visual Skills.

The second phase in the process is RECONCILIATION or how our BRAIN PROCESSES what we *thought* we saw. It is during this phase, that the mind and body must be in agreement and align themselves. When we can align the mind and body, this is what I call Reconciliation. *Def. Reconciliation: Meaning #2: get-*

ting two things to correspond. Synonym: balancing. For the purpose of this book, our objective is to reconcile the mind and body of a hitter. When the mind and body are in the same place, working together in harmony ... focus, timing, confidence, and positive results will follow.

The Reconciliation Phase is where most hitters get into trouble. They tend to make this thought process their enemy, when it could very well be their ally. The Mental Midget is way too concerned with thoughts, which do not contribute to success. Bad thoughts impede or hinder the REACTION/RESPONSE, which is our third and final phase.

Finally, the swing or the REACTION/RESPONSE has to happen. Notice that two major things have already happened before we have actually *decided* to swing the bat. Many people are skipping the first two phases of development until after HS. This is way too late! The reaction/response is what most people spend their entire life attempting to fix, while ignoring the most essential phases—phase one and two or the Read and the Reconciliation. Most teachers are breaking down only the Response or the Physical swing into 3 parts, but ignoring the 2 parts before that. Many hitters have hitting issues that are not being addressed. As hitting coaches, we are changing swings, when we should be changing minds. For most coaches, it is easier to make a judgment about a hitter based on what we can see, rather than what we should ask him.

Webster defines Mental *as follows: 1a: of or relating to the mind; specifically: of or relating to the total emotional and intellectual response of an individual to external reality.* Therefore, how we respond to the outcome of a situation or the results of our efforts will ultimately determine our thought process for future efforts. If we respond with negative emotion, we will have a negative result. If we respond by over analyzing a situation, then we self-destruct right there.

b: of or relating to intellectual as contrasted with emotional activity. c: of, relating to, or being intellectual as contrasted with overt physical activity. d: occurring or experienced in the mind. e: relating to the mind, its activity, or its products as an object of study.

Most books that have been written on *"the mental"* have been written by psychologists and have been excellent. These works have enlightened us as teachers and students of performance and helped us to understand the dynamics of thought process as it relates to learning and performance. However, when you are communicating to athletes, coaches, and other lay people, much of the doctor's jargon goes over our heads or doesn't quite translate effectively into our world and into our language. For example, an athlete will read the book or hear the presentation of a sport's psychologist and not be clear about how to implement all this new theory they have just learned. Mental skills improvement must be integrated into the instructional model, and routines must be established which can be brought to the field—even taught on the field. How is my childhood experiences and dysfunctional family relevant to my performance on the field? How can that be important to an athlete? Why does an athlete even care? Complete Game brings a new perspective to understanding and teaching the emotional game because it keeps the bat in a hitter's hands while dealing with the emotional or mental issue. If we can teach it on the field and not a classroom, we are more effective in helping athletes to translate new info **into** their game. Philosophy without implementation is useless and nothing more than a scam. We have to keep the bat and the ball involved in the mental skills teaching-process.

2

Hitters are Computers

I think the most frequently asked question by hitters at just about every level is probably, *"Why can't I hit?"* And coaches are also asking, *"Why can't they hit?"* Just because you are asking that question, it shows the passion and desire you have for improvement. If a player is: a good athlete, fundamentally sound in his approach, has a ton of God-given ability, has PASSION for the game, has an impeccable work-ethic, et cetera, et cetera, then why do they struggle? There are several reasons why they struggle. Let's take a look at the way a computer is built in order to understand the way a HITTER is built.

Many years ago developers of technology figured something out. Developers realized that computers operate better if they could duplicate human intelligence. So they duplicated human intelligence with computers. Without boring you with science, I will show you how human intelligence and computers are so much alike.

The three main elements of a computer are: Hardware, an Operating System, and Software Application. Here, I would like to show how we parallel learning and performance with how computers work.

Hardware is the computer's capability or what it can potentially do. This is for example, how much memory does it have? Does it have the ability to burn CD's or DVD's? How fast is the processor, et cetera? For hitters, Hardware is God-given ability, genetic potential, or what is developed over the coarse of time. The physical body and its capabilities, strength, athleticism, flexibility, gifts and talents are the Hardware of a hitter. This hardware can be developed. *Hardware Development* is the construction or building of the physical body. So as a hitter, your hardware lays within your ability or inability to physically perform such and such a task. This Hardware can be developed with weight training, speed, agility, quickness, and strength training. These things improve overall athletic ability which improves our Fitness, Body Strength or Hardware. As necessary as it is, if all you have is great hardware, then you will certainly struggle as an athlete and especially a hitter.

Software refers to all of the programs your computer uses to perform the actions you want it to. Software helps you get it done; it is merely information or philosophy. In other words, what you have been taught, what you believe, and what you incorporate into your hardware or swing. This could perhaps be your hitting model or philosophy.

For example, some people believe that a hitter's body should generate more rotational force rather than linear force. Then there are some who believe that there should be a combination of both. This makes a hitting coach a programmer; hitting coaches are really just installing software into hitters. So if a hitting coach or a programmer instructs you to perform a specific movement and your hardware is incapable or you just aren't strong enough, then you won't be able to do it. This is a hardware problem, because the software is not compatible to your machine. It is sort of like trying to run Microsoft Word on a calculator. It is just not a strong or fast enough machine. Let's take it a step further. Some people are comfortable creating documents in Microsoft Word and some in Word Perfect. Does it really matter which software program you use? Probably not. It is a matter of preference. It is a matter of two different types of software that can get the same task done. So if I possess any kind of ability (hardware), then I can conform to whatever hitting philosophy (software) I need to. This becomes easy when you have the right hardware and of course the right Operating System.

Finally, an **Operating System** is what is almost non-existent in sports, especially baseball and softball. It is virtually non-existent due to poor attitudes, little or no work ethic, and commitment. An example of an operating system on your computer would be Windows for your PC, or OSX for MAC users. According to Howstuffworks.com, *"the purpose of an operating system is to organize and control hardware and software so that the device it lives in behaves in a flexible but predictable way. The operating system (OS) is the first thing loaded onto the computer—without the operating system, a computer is useless."*

According to How Stuff Works, Operating Systems are made out of portable code rather than permanent physical circuits so that they can be changed or modified without having to scrap the whole device.

Examples of the Operating System for hitters would be all of the mental and emotional factors that make up a hitters mindset: Confidence, the ability to relax, concentration and focus, attitude, commitment, resilience, discipline, et cetera. Let me say here that without the proper Operating System it doesn't matter how great your hardware is or how perfect your software or hitting model is. You will not get it done! I have found that some coaches would rather be right, than to actually have their players get it done. So if their team batting average is .245, then they are okay so long as they did it their way. Well congrats on being right. You did it your way and your team still can't hit. I have also found that many coaches are teaching hitters how to have nice swings, but not how to hit. I personally would rather develop better hitters not models of what I feel the perfect swing should look like. So your bad thoughts are the viruses that distract, impede and hinder proper operation. For a better understanding of what an operating system is, see Chapter 4 (Seven Reasons Why You Can't Hit).

3

N.E.O. Complex

Def., <u>N.E.O. COMPLEX</u>: Nervy, Edgy, and Over Anxious. The N.E.O. COM-PLEX is something very common, especially amongst very gifted people. As a matter of fact, the only people who qualify for the Neo Complex are those who are extremely gifted and really do not believe it. Actually, their mental skills do not match their physical abilities. You cannot think like a number 8 batter, in the 3 hole.

Here is a great example of the NEO complex. Kelsey, who is probably one of my favorite students, is currently a Division 1 player at Kennesaw State University in Georgia. Kelsey has always had the tools for being a great hitter. She possesses strength, talent, and tremendous bat speed. Kelsey also has incredible instincts for hitting. The first day I met her, I realized I needed to help bring up her esteem, for she lacked confidence, and did not believe she could ever be a great hitter. Kelsey didn't know it then, but when I saw her take her first swing, I knew she was bound for greatness. Now she is a lot closer to believing it.

When I took on Kelsey as a student, I realized that my goals for her were not so much physical, but I needed to re-program her mind-set. I often preach that hitting is a mind-set. *(see Chapter 8, Re-Creating the Mind-Set)*.

Overcoming the N.E.O. COMPLEX is as simple as thought management or directing your thoughts. When players learn how to be in control of what their thought processes are, it becomes easier to manage their emotions, and perform in the clutch. In practice, it is important to encourage players to manage their emotional responses to adversity or negative outcomes. When players can be comfortable with being uncomfortable, then they are on their way. It begins in practice. We are now practicing a correct thought process.

Exercise:

1. A good exercise would be to have your players get together over pizza and identify the negative things that come from that little voice inside of them.

2. List them.

3. Now ask them to list something positive as a response to the negative thought.

For example:

I suck	I am the best!
I can't Hit	I Mash!
It just isn't my day	I can handle this!
I do no want to be at bat right now	Piece of cake!
This pitcher is on	So am I!

4

Why You Can't Hit? Seven Reasons

Here are some common reasons why some players just CAN'T HIT! WARNING! If you can't handle the truth, please skip this chapter.

- Limited Talent/Ability
  - No one in your family is athletic, neither are you
  - You just don't have the genes
  - Your aren't very coordinated
  - People in this category need to work twice as hard: you don't
- Weak Body Strength
  - You are not Strong
  - Need to Strength Train more diligently, but you won't
- Lack of Discipline
  - You never stick to anything, not even a video game; you probably won't even finish this book
  - Playing more than one sport and never have the time to truly commit
  - You are in denial about how good you are
  - You are also in denial about how bad you are
  - You make excuses like, *"I just don't have time"*
- Non-commitment/Inconsistent Work-Ethic
  - You have never trained year-round

- You only train a month or two before the season
- You only practice when things begin to go bad
  - No Confidence
    - Due to little or no preparation, you will never know real confidence
    - You are only confident when things are going well
    - Adversity totally breaks you
  - Low Aptitude
    - You just don't pick up things well
    - You don't get it: Truthfully, you never get it
    - It takes you a while to grasp new concepts
  - Inability to Focus
    - You are very easily distracted
    - Every little thing bothers you or takes you out of your game
    - Your emotions determine your mood

Note: How many reasons are not physical? How many reasons can you actually change? The reasons that are not physical are what make up your operating system.

Although there are many reasons why some players cannot hit, I have only listed a few. If you take a careful look at the reasons, when you improve one it enhances another. When you improve the bottom four, Talent/Ability improves. These attributes are all intertwined. Be honest with yourself and check off the things that describe you. If you are mature enough to be honest with yourself, then you have a good chance of changing. If you cannot be honest with yourself, then you will remain in denial.

Note: Many parents are signing up players for hitting instruction because they hate to see them fail. Then there are the few who sign them up because they want to continue to see them succeed. Which one are you? Training is about maintaining excellence, not always about trying to attain it.

5

T.A.G. Talent, Ability, and Gifts

Talent can be developed. That is why one can take piano or dance lessons and develop a talent for those particular arts. What is a GIFT? A gift is something that one receives without working for it. If I give you a gift, I do not expect anything back from you, therefore you do not need to pay me back. In other words, gifted people don't necessarily need to work at their crafts—they are simply GIFTED. A gift can only be given to you; that is what makes it a gift. And this gift has been **given** to them supernaturally from God. Did I say God? Yes, I did. Let's agree that God-given ability and GIFTS are synonymous. Some would argue that gifts are genetic. Gifts are never genetic, but ability sometimes can be. I have identified some gifts:

- Strong Throwing Arm
- Running Speed
- Bat Speed

If a player possesses these gifts, and is trained properly, she will no doubt improve them to where it has become a TALENT. I have seen people with weak arms, slow bats and slow foot speed; improve their form and strength in order to become talented. However, body-strength, ability to focus, discipline, and aptitude must be improved. Only one of those four attributes is physical. I OFTEN SAY, "WHEN GENES, PROPER INSTRUCTION, AND WORK ETHIC INTERSECT, A VERY SPECIAL ATHLETE WILL EMERGE."

A person with limited talent and not a lot of ability just *sucks*. I chose that word *'sucks'* purposely. I believe we dance around the truth when assessing where people really are. If someone knows they suck, they will either work harder or they will continue to suck and eventually quit. Isn't this game so much like life? Wow!

I have had more success with getting players significantly better, and in a short period of time when I raise the standard of what hard work is and the player accepts the challenge. You can only improve a player's measure of *ability to an extent*. That part that is God-given, and that part that is not, is where great teaching/learning comes in to play. You can, however, increase a player's overall *Talent*. A player's overall Talent can only be improved through dedication, commitment, and hard work. Coaches cannot teach players commitment-only parents can. That was golden, so I will repeat it. Coaches cannot teach players commitment-only parents can. If there is no commitment, there can be no significant improvement. *Until they learn to push themselves, parents have to push young athletes. We push them to sit down and study for school and they excel in school. Eventually, these habits and routines will become a part of their personality. We must also push them when it comes to sports, with regards to dedication and levels of commitment. Eventually, it will become a part of them as well (see chapter 18).*

So by improving a player's body strength and flexibility, she will then have the ABILITY to do such and such a thing. You get it? By helping one to have the discipline to maintain a consistent work ethic he will now have the ability to do X, Y, and/or Z more efficiently. So here we see how improving in the areas of strength, speed and flexibility, and improving one's work ethic, contributes to overall ABILITY. Without a consistent work ethic, a player won't work out, thus BODY STRENGTH will never happen. It is safe to then say,

"Consistent Work-Ethic + Increased Body Strength/Flexibility = Greater Ability."

So many coaches attain so much information, and are still unable to get their players better. A good question to ask yourself as a player is, *"How much better have I gotten in the past 2 years or even 1 year?"* And a good question to ask your self as a coach is, *"How much better has my players or team gotten in the past year?"* Even better, *"As a coach how much better have you gotten?"*

THE FABRIC OF THE ELITE

Who is Elite? What is that? How does one get there? Elite status is never a destination, but always a process. It is the process of ***improving upon perfection*** or continually perfecting the parts, in order to make the 'whole' better. So we focus on the process and not the result, in order to produce and maintain a growing functional organism—the ELITE ATHLETE!

Mental Fabric—The WHY! Why do they play? They play because they Love the game.

1. Love the game
2. Love the Game, Love to learn
3. Love the Game, Love to Learn, Love to compete

ELITE ATHLETES HAVE ALL THREE OF THESE ATTRIBUTES AT ALL TIMES!

6

Make-Up and Muscle: Form and Power

How important is form? *How does my swing look? Am I dropping my back shoulder? Is it perfect?* Please! Shut up already! Form is most important in the early development of a hitter. I have found that although form is crucial to great consistency in timing and power, a player's infatuation with form can and almost always leads to failure, choking, and the inability to achieve peak performance. I believe that too many hitters are in love with their swings and pitchers in love with their deliveries. Just way too much *MAKE-UP!* Stop being such a perfectionist!

The over-emphasis of form should be the main focus of off-season training only. Yes. There must be an off-season. Competing year-round is quite fun, but it hinders the growth process and development of skills and instincts.

How important is strength? *I don't want/need a personal trainer. I am training with this guy at my local gym that never played baseball or softball? I go to the gym already.* Those are the common excuses. If 100 hitters have perfect swings, only 25 of them can actually hit. If your swing is perfect, then you have a nice swing. This doesn't mean you can hit. You are simply a bad hitter, with a great swing! We must combine proper hitting movements with body strength and flexibility.

Don't get me wrong—I love a pretty swing. But I will take a strong hitter with an ugly swing, over a weak hitter with a pretty swing any day. I have said this in the past and pissed some people off, but I maintain that I will not work with a hitter who is not enrolled in a good strength program. Strength is just way too important. And because I make it important, my students make it important. I would say that every single one of my students who are at the Division 1 level have had a personal trainer throughout HS and have quit other sports by the end of their freshman year. Thus my students are having tremendous success. So when people come up to me and say, *"You've done a great job with so and so,"* I can honestly say it is due to their hard work and not because I am so wonderful.

I declare that hitting is a mentality as well as an attitude. Hitting is a mind-set. Commitment is also a mind-set. Many players, especially in the northeast, don't quit basketball, field hockey or volleyball until it is too late. If that time had been spent on Proper Strength Training, things would be very different. College might even be discounted for them. But the number one excuse for players not training year-round is they are *'playing basketball to stay in shape for softball or baseball.'* That just doesn't make sense to me. Try studying English in preparation for your next math test!

7

Making a Connection

o o o o o o o o o o o o o o o o o o o o o o o o o o o o o o o o o

"I've had a chance to coach women and men, and the one thing I do know is men have to play good to feel good; women have to feel good to play good," ... "And so you've got to spend a lot of your time getting young kids to feel good about themselves.

—Mike Candrea, Univ. of Arizona, Softball

KNOW YOUR HITTERS. As a coach or instructor, the ability to make a connection with your student is a gift in itself. How does a coach or instructor make a connection with a player? First of all, if you are a frustrated or burnt out coach, you should either quit or take some time off. It is a lot easier to communicate to players who like you. Are you likeable? Do your players hate your guts? Are you miserable? Are you always pointing out the negative and never congratulating the positive? Have you ever played the game you are coaching? Do you play favorites? Have you created clicks on your team? Do you foster an atmosphere where athletes can become more teachable? Do you at least have average people skills?

I find it unnatural for a coach to give instruction to a hitter without having a conversation with players to find out how they are doing in school. How is their personal life? What are their hobbies and interests? Are they dating anyone? Did they hang out last night? Et cetera. Feedback is so important. Establishing a relationship and a degree of comfort is very important. Some of my players are so accustomed to talking to me, that they come for a hitting lesson and begin to talk without me asking any questions. I find myself learning from my students as much as they learn from me.

So this brings me to my next point: I have found that I can learn more about how to help a hitter by engaging them in conversation, than from seeing their swing! As an instructor, I like to first make an assessment of whom I am working with? What is their personality? Does she have a consistent work ethic? What are her goals? How passionate is she? And what kind of hitter is he? How do she handle criticism? How does he handle failures? What type of hitter would he like to become? How crazy are her parents? Who is his favorite hitter to watch? Does he even watch the sport? Do she even love the sport? Is she a perfectionist?

Allow me to pose the question: Are hitters born or made? Are hitters developed from the inside out or the outside in? How much is nature and how much is nurture? I guess I'm asking myself that question. See Chapter 16.

"Its all about the software, not only the hardware."

IBM maintained that hardware was everything, but along came a smarter guy named Bill Gates. He realized that if the focus was on software or information and programming, he could help hardware run more efficiently. Well it's the same for training hitters for high-level success. At some point, it won't matter how good a player is if they're not running the proper software or if the mental facilities are not functioning properly. So hitters can be made from the inside out or/and from the outside in.

There are 2 kinds of hitters:

    a) Those who CAN hit

    b) Those who CAN'T hit

Now that I have made this determination, it is important for me to find out what the situation is.

There are 2 situations is training:

    a) Those who <u>don't</u> <u>have</u> <u>it</u> and <u>want</u> <u>to</u> <u>get</u> <u>it</u>

    b) Those who <u>do</u> <u>have</u> <u>it</u> and <u>want</u> <u>to</u> <u>maintain</u> <u>it</u>

And the bottom line is, we should all strive to gain more.

8

Re-Creating The Mindset

o o o o o o o o o o o o o o o o o o o o o o o o o o o o o o o o o o

'Hitters must learn to unlearn everything that they have learned.'

"SEE IT AND HIT IT." Read and React or Read and Respond. Probably the best in-game advice you can give a hitter. Back in chapter one, we looked at the Three R's, but here we only see two. That is because most people don't understand what happens in between the read and the response. So what do we do? We ignore it. Then we say, *This game is so mental.* But we never prepare our players for the mental conflict. Below I have outlined 7 issues that we can explore throughout this chapter.

What happens in between read and respond/react? The reconciliation phase of the swing is crucial to the read and is also crucial to the reaction or response. When the mind and body are in the same place at the same time, this is what contributes to consistency and excellence for maximum in-game focus. Many hitters are somewhere else mentally while their body is left to perform the task without the proper assistance of the brain. Where do hitters go when their minds are not "one" with the body? Many of them are still on the last pitch or AB or discouraged by the error they made last inning or even last game. They are certainly not involved in the process. This is a classic case of mis-management of emotions. Emotions are in control here and not the player. As a coach, you cannot have a player with a lot of responsibility in this mindset. To be specific, if your short-stop, pitcher or catcher is a mental midget, you are in for a long season.

Train the brain to block out distractions. In drills, we can train players to think in terms what is next. Or what is the next pitch? I always tell my players, "It is always about the next pitch." Or, "You are only as good as your next swing or AB, or ground ball." If they are in the present with an anticipation of what is next, then they cannot be looking backwards. Coaches can implement drills where things are happening fast. For example, in soft toss or tee drills, force your players to keep the same face on bad swings. I coached an 11U travel baseball team some years ago. I had a rule. No crying! Anyone who cried or threw a piece of equipment would have to come out of the game. By mid-season, we were so focused it was incredible. That same team went on to turn 21 double plays and something like 12 shutouts. Our in-game focus was unparalleled. Eventually it will become normal to maintain a consistent attitude through the good times and bad. It begins with how we practice.

Baseball and softball are relatively slow games. And often times, things we did in the first innings will linger into the third, fourth, or fifth inning. In other sports, whatever happened in the first quarter is quickly forgotten by the two-minute warning in the fourth quarter. Helping players to identify CD's or common distractions will assist in overcoming them. (See Chapter 10, Turning the Page).

What are the CD's or Common Distractions for hitters? <u>Define Distraction</u>: *A condition or state of mind in which the attention is diverted from an original focus or interest. Diversion of the attention. An obstacle of the attention.* See Chapter 13, Common Distractions.

Can distractions be eliminated? No. Distractions will always exist. But we can eliminate the way distractions affect us. We eliminate distractions by accepting them as necessary elements of the game and conditioning the mind to ignore them. Complaining about distractions or even responding to them only magnifies them. We go around, through, under, or over our obstacles. This is a mindset, and must be incorporated into our practice.

How do we help hitters to improve focus? It goes back to how practice. Practice makes permanent. *"We are what we repeatedly do. Excellence then, is not an act, but a habit."* Most practices are a joke. Most practices are way too long. I know of teams who claim to be high level, but they bring a different hitting coach in every 2 weeks. MY GOD! There is no routine and there is no sense of intensity. Practice is nothing like the game. Practices are way too laid back. Your individual and team focus will be as good as it is in your practice. Whatever and however you practice, it will become permanent. See chapter 9, Improving In-Game Focus.

How can we get hitters to focus longer? By establishing routines in practice and training is the simplest way to increase focus. Athletes become more comfortable with routines. Pre-game warm-ups should be routine and post-game routines should also be established.

How can we help hitters to become more selective?
See DVD for Hitting Drills.

How can we help hitters to establish disciplined hitting zones?
See DVD for Hitting Drills.

ARE HITTING ISSUES ALWAYS PHYSICAL?

> *"On the highest level, 80% of hitting is talent and the remaining 20% is form/mechanics. This is only after our swing is real good."*

Hitting issues are rarely physical. A lot of hitters will make an out and ask, *"What am I doing wrong?"* Many coaches will see a hitter make an out and immediately have a solution as to why that hitter made an out. Could it be perhaps that no one can get a hit every time up. If she bats .400, then she has to make an out 6 out of 10 times. Outs happen. And it is usually because of what the thought process is or isn't. Not always the physical process.

HITTERS WITH THE HIGHEST APTITUDES ARE GENERALLY AUDIO IN THEIR LEARNING

<u>Define Aptitude</u>: *An inherent ability, as for learning; A talent. Awareness in learning and understanding. A natural or acquired capacity or ability.*

People generally learn in three ways. So there are three primary ways or modalities in which we all learn: Auditory, Visual, and Kinetic. Let's call them Hearing, Seeing, and Feeling. There are more people who learn by Feeling/Kinetic than any of the three primary modalities. Great teachers should have the ability to say it and demonstrate it. Teachers must also be creative enough to help athletes to feel it as well.

9

Improving In-Game Focus

IMPROVING IN-GAME FOCUS WITH SPECIFIC DRILLS

Incorporate certain drills into the workout where the stress of game-like conditions are present and forces the student to focus their thoughts on particular objectives rather than their surrounding distractions.

I have noticed that many coaches are not detail oriented and simply put their players through drills for the sake of keeping them occupied. These types of coaches can run an organized practice well, but I am not sure how purposeful the sessions are for the personal development of the players. In my soon to be released DVD, I am going to outline 12 different types of drills that can improve your player's in-game focus.

You will get a kick out of this one. I was conducting a clinic for youth baseball in my hometown over this past winter and I was working with the 9 year-olds. There were two players in particular who actually stood out to me as not being very athletic but I could tell that they loved the game. Anyhow, I had just covered the proper way to address fly balls and was conducting a competitive exercise for tracking down fly balls, and catching them with one hand (the glove hand with no glove). This is a drill I stole from Jessica Mendoza, where we use the bouncy tennis balls in order to make catching more difficult. One really has to be focused in order to master this. Would you believe that these two players actually won the contest? When I found out that one of the players was a chess mater and the other an honor student, I was not surprised. We cannot deny that focus is focus, whether in chess, in the classroom, or in the game. The better athletes did not have the focus to get it done. Their inability to perform was due to lack of focus.

Define <u>Focused</u>: 1. *a state or condition permitting clear perception or understanding.* *2. CG definition, the opposite of distracted.*

Define <u>Concentration</u>: *the fixing of close undivided attention. A directive of the attention or of the mental faculties toward a single object. Complete attention: Intense effort.*

Most players, who struggle with focus/concentration on the field, will struggle with focus/concentration off the field. Players with the inability to focus/concentrate can never be consistent. These are your athletes with tremendous amounts of potential, but never make it out of the bottom of the order. Or the kid who could be shortstop, but you will only trust him at 2B or in the outfield.

How I develop players to improve their in-game concentration goes back to how I train them. If your practices and pre-game rituals are a joke, please do not expect your players to be serious or focused in the game. Practice and training should constantly challenge your athletes. Practice and pre-game should never be laid back. They must be as intense as the games, and sometimes more. Players must be made to block out the things that don't matter when it is time to perform. When SHOWTIME is here, nothing else matters except getting it done. Practices and individual training must be geared towards Developing the proper ways of thinking, which is a skill critical for in-game success.

In practice, we challenge players to focus on fine objectives and strengthening weaknesses. For example, hitters are given drills, with specific objectives. We can measure a player's ability to focus in-game, by how they accomplish specific tasks. Most players would rather work on things they do well, or begin to wander away from the objective of the drill. This is more fun for them, but not always the best thing for improving in-game focus.

We usually challenge our players to memorize what every batter in the order did in each of their AB's. Sounds difficult, but it isn't. I have met 9 year-old poker players who memorize what cards have hit the table and know what cards have not. It is a matter of improving your concentration skills. To go a step further, memorizing what pitch the hitter hit and where he hit it. Concentration is a skill; therefore we can improve upon it. I will turn around and ask the bench what is the count in order to keep them *"in the game."* Another good one for keeping players in the game is having the bench to yell "bunt" when the batter is bunting or "going" when a player is stealing. Any player who has ever played for me knows we have stiff penalties for anyone who does not participate in this; I call it the choir. We run till someone throws up. That is how important being "in the game" is to me. If I can keep them in the game, we can be a more focused and winning team.

You would be surprised how many professional athletes forget how many outs there are when they are on the bases. I saw Bernie Williams, a seasoned veteran, almost get doubled up at second on an infield fly to shortstop, with one out and the bases loaded. Where was he?

Donovan Mitchell, who is currently the Rookie Ball Manager for the NY Mets, is a personal friend who I trained in his pro ball days with the Houston Astros. Knowing that Donovan is an experienced teacher of the game and Player Development personality, I asked him what are some of the things he does with the Kingsport Mets in order to improve in-game focus.

> *"practices are set in game mode ... instead of throwing a kid 50 pitches and having him hit it and explain to him what he is doing wrong, we throw him 25 and have him explain what he is looking to do in certain situations and why. What pitch is he looking for in certain situations and having him work on his discipline to allow certain pitches go by in order to get a better one ... no longer are we just practicing catching a ground ball but we are practicing ground balls pretending there is a fast runner or the tying run is on 3B. We work cutoff relays using a fast runner on base and slow runner at the plate or vice versa. We also hit the ball hard or soft and make the players have to make decisions just like they would in games. Having players practice at game speed and having to go through a mental checklist before the play even develops prepares them for the game."*

10

Turning the Page

Failure is a necessary part of the game. Can you handle that? If you find yourself succeeding more than you are failing, especially in hitting, then what's the point? Where is the challenge? The thing that makes ripping a line-drive base hit up the middle so rewarding is the fact that it is so difficult to do. This is what motivates us to work harder and learn about our own personal process. If it were that easy and you could bat .750 with your eyes closed, then you could not know work ethic. Of course, we never dwell on the failed attempts, but we certainly learn from them in order to be successful in our next attempt. Losing is the same. We definitely learn more from losing than winning in the long run. The wonderful thing about failing is we live to try again. There is another AB, another game, another day, another season. Isn't that great!

Define <u>Resilience</u>: *The capability to recover or adjust easily to failure or change especially caused by undesired results or stress.*

Below is a real email from a player who doesn't know it yet but is probably one of the top softball prospects in the country:

Rob,
I am very frustrated right now with my hitting. Today we played at the one-day Pennsbury tournament; I went 1 for 9 (not at all good). I had 2 ground balls, one strike out swinging, 5 pop-ups and one hit up the middle. I came home and watched the DVD and made some notes but I don't get why I am not hitting. I'm so frustrated at this point that I don't even wanna play softball anymore. I cry sometimes when I come home because I feel like I did so bad. I used to be such a good hitter and I don't know what's wrong. Maybe I'm thinking too much about it and have it drilled into my head that I can't hit the ball and that's why I'm not, I don't know. Since I've changed my swing I've been struggling a lot and was wondering if it's ever going to click ... I don't want to perform

badly on the team and not get asked to play again next year, and I don't want to go to Texas and California (and travel all that way and spend all that money and time) and not perform in front of the college coaches. Maybe I am just thinking too much, but it's really hard to not think about anything when all you think about is trying to hit the ball (if that made any sense at all). Maybe I just need to work harder on the hitting and do more reps here. Please email me back and try to talk me off the ledge ...

Thanks,
Katherine

My Response:

Got your email. It is good to know that you have such a passion for the game and you are hungry for success. I have some thoughts in which I would like you to read through every day:

I want you to practice learning how to TURN THE PAGE. I want you to Practice learning how to FOCUS on WHAT IS NEXT and not WHAT HAS ALREADY HAP-PENED. Your fear of failure is not unusual but you are too good to be afraid of failing. Especially since failure is a big part of softball at every level.

College coaches want to see you how you handle failure as well as success. It is easy to be confident when everything is good, but can you show confidence during the bad times. College coaches focus more on the process and not the results. They need to make projections on where you will be in 3 years, and not necessarily where you are currently. Right now, you are becoming a great hit-ter. And every great hitter has to learn how to fail. You haven't learned that yet. A-Rod knows how to fail. I remember when Derek Jeter had a long slump where he learned how to fail. He smiled in the dugout and just played great defense until his hitting came around.

I know you love this game. But remember that is what it is—A GAME! So the pressure that you put on yourself is enormous. You are only in 10th grade. You still haven't had a full off-season with me yet in order to work towards real per-fection of the movements. When I watch your AB's I always say to myself, "the coaches are gonna love her." Your swing is very good and you have a lot of ability. If I saw your potential on the 1st day, then they certainly will. College coaches know who the great ones are and so does Jim. That is why you are on the team.

We haven't really made changes to your swing, however we have made adjust-ments. I need you to hang in there and continue to work. Replace your negative thoughts with positive thoughts. Once you learn how to cope with these little struggles, you will realize true greatness. You are going through exactly what every player has to go through in their lives. It is called adversity. Pass this test and you will look back and smile on this. In the meantime, go to my website www.complete-game.net and read all of my past blogs in order to see how I have addressed some of the issues you are dealing with now. Softball is a great game, and you are doing fine. Its all about the process, the results will come.

p.s. Do me a favor, write down all the negative thoughts that go through your mind before, during, or even after a game. Then write down something positive next to it in order to counter the negative thought. When you are done, email me the list.

Sincerely,
ROB CREWS

Now here is an email I received seven months later from the same player:

Rob,

We won our county game today in the second round against Governor Livingston and Capri Catalano. We won 1-0 ... I hit a home run, the only run and RBI in the game, and Capri only gave up one hit ... my home run. It was a good game today and I think that's one of the first times I've hit off her so I'd deff say I'm improving.

Our next county game is the semi-final this Friday at the Linden complex. I'll keep you updated.

—Kat

If you analyze both emails and pay attention to the language, you will see that both emails are the same. Most players are outcome driven. Positive outcomes make them feel confident, and negative outcomes make them feel defeated. Before Kat goes to college, she will grow into the realization of *UNCONDI-TIONAL CONFIDENCE* (see Chapter 12). Athletes in their emotion, can only see themselves where they are. They usually do not see past how they feel or their current circumstances. This is the process of maturation that everyone will experience, whether in life or sport.

I have found that most players who have the capability to bounce back from adversity or especially failure, possess an attribute most necessary for success called **resilience**. An athlete that is resilient is one who has the ability to turn the page. He or she is capable of managing past failures and successes well. So many players take their last pitch, their last swing, their last AB, or even their last game into the next one. Whether it was a good AB or bad AB, we are only as good as our next one. If you don't write down anything from this book, please write that one down. I will say it again, *"You are only as good as your next opportunity."* Sometimes the worst thing a hitter can do is hit a homerun.

I recently had dinner with the starting shortstop and second baseman of a major Division I softball team. The majority of the conversation, they both focused on everything they hated about their situation. The coach, the coach's philosophy, the favoritism, and the lesbianism were among the things that made them uncomfortable. There was a long list of factors they had allowed to affect their attitude and ultimately their performances. They were hindered by their frustration and inability to be resilient. As an athlete, you cannot focus on how you want things to be, but accept the challenges of discomfort and use it as motivation to fuel your personal fire. The situation may not always change, but you can certainly change.

A resilient athlete can go into any situation, no matter how negative and succeed. To tell you the truth, I get nervous when I know an athlete is college-bound or next level-bound and has never gone through any adversity. Never had a long slump, an injury, a bad year, or bad month for that matter. An athlete is never prepared for the next level, without first being tested. How one handles failure, ultimately determines the potential height of their success. Can you name something besides life itself that has more failure/adversity involved than baseball or softball? I can't.

If I were a professional scout for a major league team, I would love to see the recruit strike out three times, then see the very next game, just to see how they how they bounce back. I already know the player has talent to play at the next level—that is why I am recruiting him. But I do not know how she manages failures. True character and athletic greatness lies within your ability to get up after a great fall. Resilience!

I had the pleasure of coaching a young lady named Lauren Gibson, who is verbally committed to attend and play at the University of Tennessee. She is from Maryland and a fine hitter. Lauren is focused, disciplined, and so talented. She is small in body, but possesses tremendous focus and unbelievable power. Anyway, Lauren played with Team NJ this past Fall of 2006, where I helped out with the hitters. The team was mostly comprised of 9th and 10th graders and we competed against 18U Gold teams. Let me tell you this young lady put on a hitting clinic for the entire fall. It was amazing. However, I only really knew the type of player Lauren was when I saw her fail. The way she handled it with such maturity. Only great hitters handle failure the way she did. In our final tourney, she went hitless for about 3 games. Of course she was frustrated, but really managed it well. Then she breaks out with a game tying two-run homerun to the opposite field. It was just clutch! I am convinced that you will only know the great ones by how they handle the bad times.

"I like players that have great body language through the good times and the bad."

—*Tim Walton, Head Coach, Florida Gators Softball*

11

Multiple Chef Syndrome

Here's something to thing about: If I am in the kitchen baking a cake with two or three other chefs, and I put the sugar in and then chef #2 puts the sugar in also. And because chef #3 doesn't know that sugar has already been added, puts even more sugar in. We now have a disgusting cake that is just way too sweet. It is the same way with hitters who have more than one batting coach. It becomes a problem—especially when the two coaches are not in communication with each other, or worse, not in agreement. The worse thing a coach can do is to belittle the other coach, especially in front of the student (even if you think the other one is off). You will lose credibility with the student who will sense your insecurities.

This is such a delicate issue and almost everyone I know must deal with this at some point in his or her career. Truthfully, it is probably one if the biggest distractions or hindrances I can think of. I had a player who was no doubt one of the best players I ever coached. His name is Mike. At the time, Mike was a freshman and played outfield for a Division 1 program in the Northeast. Mike was about 5'9" with tremendous power and speed. I knew Mike was a power hitter and that is what got him to such a high level of play. Because of Mike's size and running speed, his coaches decided to put him into a crouch and change him into a contact hitter. This really affected Mike's aggressiveness and confidence. Soon after, Mike went from batting lead off to seventh, and then ninth, and eventually he was out of the lineup.

So one evening I get a phone call from Mike's mother who was extremely concerned about him. Apparently he was depressed and didn't want to play baseball anymore. In fact, she urged me to call him at the hotel where his team was staying during a road trip. He had told her he was thinking of leaving the hotel and just walking home. That would have been a 300-mile walk. Of course I called him immediately. I basically told him, *"If you ever get back into the lineup again, you needed to show them why you should be batting 3rd in the order. Just spit on the plate and do it your way. Be the player that you are? What have you got to lose?"*

29

After that conversation Mike proceeded to go like 16 for his next 19 AB's with 3 homers in a game. He also tied a school record for 7 or 8 hits in a game, and was named conference player of the week.

Here's another scenario:

Julie is a junior in HS and has been training with me for over 4 years. Julie has just been selected to play on the west coast's most premiere college showcase team, the A Team. She is so excited. Little does Julie know that the skills that made Julie attractive as a player, would later prove not to be good enough for the A Team. The A Team's batting coach does not like her approach to hitting. He believes that it is either his way or the highway. In fact, Julie is hitting the ball hard, but the A Team's batting coach is very stubborn about his beliefs. And is negative with her about her swing mechanics. So much so, that it has affected her confidence and she doesn't know what to believe. Julie is at a very familiar cross-road. Now it is one thing if what you were doing with your former coach is not working for you. But it is another, if it is working. Eventually she will begin to believe that what she is doing doesn't work. Four questions arise in this situation:

Question #1: Who do I listen to?

Those who have to ask themselves this question are on their way to taking themselves out. They will ultimately die a slow death. Whether it is hitting or pitching, one must be certain about who they trust as an instructor. I have a saying, *"Eat the meat and spit out the bones."* In other words, listen to your new coach or your 'other' coach, no matter how clue-less he or she is. I am sure they are well intended. And after you listen to them, pick out what information will help you, and disregard what will hurt you. Meat will always help you, and bones will always choke you. Be respectful and learn how to ignore the negative commentary. Don't be so emotional. Pretend they're your parents, and disregard everything they say. *Just kidding!*

Question #2: To what extent should I seek consultation outside of home-base?

I don't believe in having more than one coach for specific instruction beyond a certain age. If you are a player with a certain skill level and passion, you must work with one person or within one philosophy. So many parents have these young athletes all over the place. That can be dangerous and a certain hindrance to proper development.

I recall having a conversation with a certain Division I baseball coach. He stopped by my office one day just to chit-chat. He coached Division I baseball for over 20 years and as he was about to retire he told me a story about 3 players whom he had recruited but would be under the tutelage of the new head coach. As sort of a mentor to the new coach, his instructions were, *"not to give these three players any instruction. These are your best hitters, but if you fool with their swings and **get into their heads**, they will lose their confidence and be unproductive for you."* So of course, in their zeal, the new coaches went ahead and attempted to make these guys better. The end result was these players hitting almost 200 points lower in batting average.

My point is, some of these players just have too much knowledge, and are over-coached. Coaches have to begin to know who to leave alone and how much information a player needs to know. Players are doing way to much thinking and not enough performing. Leave them alone! Let me share something with you. I will not have a conversation with certain players about mechanics during the season, especially if they have trained in the off-season. And if a player has not trained in the off-season, how can they realistically implement new concepts during the season if they haven't spent a significant amount of time working on it? This is true depending upon the level of the player and their ability to make adjustments.

Recently, one of my students gave me her college softball coach's cell phone number and asked me to call him regarding some of her hitting issues. This is a PAC-10 team, and she is the number no. 3 hitter. He was secure enough to chat with me regarding the adjustments he wanted to see in her approach. I thought it was great dialogue and I wish more coaches were that awesome.

You would be surprised to know how many Division I College Baseball and Softball coaches have brought in "hitting people," to work with their hitters in order to establish, enhance, or compliment the team hitting model. Either the coaching staff is not very knowledgeable in hitting or feels that one person dedicated to hitting only will help the team to reach another level. Many of these programs are top 20 teams. If it is good enough for major league baseball, then I guess it should be good enough for the elite college level. I just cannot imagine Joe Torre trying to be the manager of the Yankees, and the batting coach also.

Question #3: How do I communicate my frustration/confusion to an insecure coach?

In a very courteous and diplomatic fashion, let your coach know that you would like some time to work through your issues (perhaps your coach needs time to work through his/her own issues). Explain that you have worked extremely hard at what you are currently doing, and you are comfortable with what you are doing. More importantly, you are confident in what you are doing. If your coach is still too insecure to allow someone else who may be more effective in helping you, continue to eat the meat and spit out the bones! Perhaps you could even ask your current coach to call your batting coach in order to better understand why you are doing what you are doing.

On the flip side, there have been times when I just couldn't get through to a hitter—no, I shouldn't lie. But if there ever would come a time where I could not help a hitter, I hope I would be secure enough to even recommend her to someone else. I always keep in mind that it is not about me, it is about the player's own individual development. Coaches, just because you read a book or bought the latest video, it doesn't make you this great hitting coach. You cannot and should not cookie cut your hitters. What works for one hitter may not necessarily work for another. This is so true, especially at the competitive-teenage level and into the collegiate and professional levels. At the highest level, it almost never works that way. I have some hitters who are more linear than others. Some hitters are just who they are.

Question #4: What do I believe?

There is a way to coach players who have personal coaches without belittling the other coach. We never want to create confusion or frustration in the player. And we most certainly don't want our hitters to lose their aggressiveness because of major swing adjustments. Belittling another coach might make you feel better, but it doesn't make you better. This fosters anxiety within your player.

12

Confidence is a Mindset?

Confidence is a result of routine and preparation. Confidence is the belief in your skill or ability to be successful. For example: your ability to hit with two strikes, pitch with a three-0 count, or your ability to handle pressure.

- How hard have you worked?
- How strong are you?
- How prepared are you?
- Do you expect to win? Or do you hope to win?
- Do you doubt yourself?

Some athletes expect to fail, and of course this causes them to fail. This also boosts future failure.

Confidence affects our F.A.T. (see F.A.T.)

Where does CONFIDENCE come from?

- Past Success and Victories
- Work ethic/preparation
- Positive Coaches Support
- Peer's Success
- Environment-conditions
- Odds on favorite
- Positive Parental Support

BUILDING CONFIDENCE

"… if big leaguers and US Olympians have to train to be good, who are you not to …"

Confidence is all about preparation. That is why I do not believe in bad BP. Imagine taking a final exam, you have not studied for. You would not be very confident taking that exam. Now imagine taking a final exam you actually studied for. Then you would be very confident going into that exam. A player's confidence is rooted in their preparation. Proper preparation should be apart of a routine. A routine should be pre-game, in-game, and post-game rituals that occur on a regular basis. Pre-game routines are important. What people call superstitions, I call pre-game rituals. If you have to eat a PB and J sandwich before each game or listen to a certain song before the game, this is all good stuff. I used to drink a milkshake the night before every game. It was just something I had to do.

UNCONDITIONAL CONFIDENCE

What is UNCONDITIONAL CONFIDENCE? Is this even possible? Well basically, it is easy to be confident when everything is going well. The most difficult thing to do is maintain confidence during the struggle. How can I help players to realize true confidence during the low points of the season? Remember, there is a season within the season. Apples don't fall off the tree all year round. Therefore you will have some rough terrain. Unconditional Confidence is a result of managing our thoughts. Believe it or not, thought travels. People tend to hold thoughts. I am teaching players how to allow thoughts to move into and eventually through their minds. When the negative thought comes into your mind, just let it keep passing through. That is something you have to train yourself to do. I have found that many parents and some coaches often foster negative thinking by reminding players about what has already happened. This is teaching players how to hold on to the past. Or hold on to the thought. You cannot do that in this sport: it is too much of a game of failure. A large percentage of people cannot handle failure, so we have lacrosse. If a player wanted to turn the page, some parents and coaches wouldn't let them anyway. They would never let them forget about mistakes and past failures.

There is a way to articulate past mistakes into learning experiences without making it a negative conversation. Here is an example, *"2 outs, runners on 2ⁿᵈ and 3ʳᵈ, and there's a ground ball hit to second base. The second baseman fields it cleanly and comes up and throws a bullet to home plate. The runner on third scores, the run-*

ner on second goes to third and of course the batter is safe at first base." Here is a positive response, "shortstop comes over to the second base-man and pats him on the back and says turn the page, or no problem, we got this." Coach yells out that it is okay, we'll get the next one. Another coach yells out something funny, we all laugh it off and we concern ourselves with what happens next.

What that player DOES NOT need to experience, is the silent treatment, or see his Dad walk away from the fence shaking his head or his coach throw up his hands. How can a player learn to re-focus with this going on? Now you see how we breed mental midgets. Because we have coaches and parents who are mental midgets. Take a look around when you go to a little league game; this is where it all begins. The good, the bad, and the ugly are all learned at the Youth Levels.

Can someone be OVERCONFIDENT? Without a doubt. Overconfidence is really a false sense of confidence. Athletes who are overconfident think their abilities are more than they really are, but hardly believe it. We should be confident without underestimating the capabilities of our opponent.

THE SWAGGER: Practicing Attitude and Focus

He thinks he's all that! She has such a cocky attitude! He is so conceited. She is good, real good, maybe a little arrogant though! The correct Mind-Set is something that we have to put on. Could Clark Kent fly without a cape? In order for Clark Kent to fly, he always had to put on his cape. As super athletes or elite athletes, we must always put on that SWAGGER! I often wonder how athletes can become more mature in the game if they do not practice their thought process. For example, so many athletes get upset during practice and have negative comments about their performance and focus on the wrong things during the workout. It is almost hilarious.

In sports, we often talk about the swagger, but I am not sure everyone knows what that is. The swagger is something that you absolutely must/can practice. Answers.com defines <u>swagger</u>: *1. To walk or conduct oneself with an insolent or arrogant air; strut. 2. To brag; boast.* In fact, we practice how to walk, having the right ATTITUDE even after a strike out or an error. Players should practice walking up to the batter's box. Player's should practice how they carry themselves. There should be something about you that is intimidating to the opponent. Let me give you an example of the swagger.

I grew up in what many people would say is a tough neighborhood. Whenever I would have to venture to the other side of the city to visit friends, it would be a little strange and sometimes scary entering some of the buildings. In one particular instance, I had to walk into a building where there were some guys a bit older and much bigger than I. They were sitting on the front steps, smoking cigarettes and drinking beer, cursing and talking loud. I had to walk by them in order to enter the building. I had to put on my best swagger in order to not appear intimidated. Had I shown any signs of weakness, they would have sensed it, and perhaps bullied me. There are some players who have a look of fear and intimidation on them and it really gives the opponent more confidence. When does 'looking the part' become true for you as a player? We should all look the part! When does acting as though you are, even you are not, become real for you? We should all act like we are THE MAN! Or WOMAN! Even when we don't feel that we are. It is a matter of getting into character. Natasha Watley, former NCAA Female Athlete of the year and USA Gold medalist, is most certainly an athlete who exudes that air of confidence on the field. I asked Natasha if she would expound on the Swagger and she said, *"I think your swagger is the most important thing that can set you apart from your opponent. Having a swagger gives you a presence; and having such a presence can be intimidating ... even on the days you don't have it, you can 'fake it till you make it' ... the swagger can breed confidence in yourself and your teammates."*

GETTING INTO CHARACTER

"Life is like a curveball, learn to adjust."

Getting into character is something people talk about in show business. However in sports, we say we're putting on our GAME FACE. But we are, indeed getting into character. One can be a pussycat off the field, and then as fierce as a tiger on the field. The truth is, in any kind of performance, the performer has to get mentally and emotionally prepared. Football players yell and scream in the locker room. Surgeons have to scrub in. Scrubbing in is not only about sterilization but it symbolizes clean thoughts as well. It is preparation for the pressure performing the surgery or saving a life. Trial lawyers have to get into character as well. So it is not only athletes. One must have the ability to perform, even when things off the field may not be going well. If a surgeon, trial lawyer, boxer, or actress would allow their personal struggles or problems to interfere, then they are no longer emotionally or mentally fit to do the job at the level of expectation. No matter what is going on, you must have the ability to get into character. Athletes are people too, and certainly not exempt from life's trials and tribulations. Personal adversity is a natural part of our human growth process. If you have never experienced personal adversity, then keep on living ... you will. Sports can be your outlet, temporary escape, or perhaps even your therapy. But whatever the case, when you step on the field, court, stage, or platform, its SHOWTIME! It's time to do what you have prepared yourself for. It's time to do what you love to do. For me, I was always a better player, when my life was full of turmoil off the field. Baseball was my passion. The game was apart of me. Without the game, I don't know what I would have done in the spring and summers of my life. When I asked, Serena Settlemier, 2006 Big 12 Player of the Year, she maintains, *"my focus on the field was intense ... I never heard the crowd and never showed emotion ... Focus is something every athlete has to maintain to be successful ... Many lose sight of their focus or their priorities. I lost mine through adversity. I also regained better focus through adversity."*

13

CD's: Common Distractions

○ ○

"Most distractions come from being away from the park ... with some guys it can be women, not eating right, not getting enough sleep, video games and the internet ... Some are away from home for the first time and have to deal with issues of being home sick. Some just don't know how to take care of themselves.

—*Donovan Mitchell, Player Development, NY METS*

Distracted is the opposite of Focused. So we are either focused or distracted. In this chapter I have outlined some of the Common Distractions, or factors that can hinder focus. CD's or Common Distractions are like viruses. Distractions, such as financial and school problems, are what cause our *programs* to operate incorrectly and corrupt our computer's memory.

PARALYSIS BY ANALYSIS: OVER ANALYTICAL, OVER COACHED

This player has way too much info and is definitely over-coached. She gets up to the plate and thinks about everything she has to do. If you fall into this category, guess what? There are about 132 different muscle movements in a swing. Go ahead and try to concern yourself with all of them—in a game no less. Good luck failing!

Some players just need to be left alone. So many coaches are over-coaching. You have players who batted .450 last season and your current team batting average is under .250 yet you feel the need to change the .400 hitter's swing. What is that? It is perfectly okay for someone to be a good hitter and it not be because of you!

I have been recently working with Team New Jersey, an elite softball club team comprised of players from all over the east coast who just went to California and went 6-1, and hit the most homeruns in the tournament. My goal for this team as a hitting coach was to work with their current swings (which are not broken) make adjustments (not changes), and fine tune their mindsets, making them into more mature hitters. There are some girls I literally ran from. I wouldn't talk to them about swing mechanics. What makes a great hitting coach, is knowing when to implement change, and knowing when not to. Everyone does not have to hit the same way. As a young coach who is learning new things all the time, it is natural to want to teach every hitter everything you know to be right. But just because it's right doesn't mean it will work for everyone. I find this to be so true, especially with high-level college players and professionals. Most of them can hit any way you teach them—whether right or wrong, they will hit anyhow.

It is also important to know what to say to a player during the game without causing him to lose aggressiveness at the plate. Some coaches are giving hitting clinics during the game. You cannot expect a player to make drastic changes in their swing mechanics during an AB. You can, however, remind them of something you have already talked about prior. Perhaps you can make a suggestion in between innings or even between a double-header, but during the game is difficult for a lot of hitters. This is a major distraction and probably the most dangerous CD

INJURIES

> "Being out of basketball taught me a lot. I watched from the sidelines and learned a lot," she said. "I learned that in an instant the game I love could be taken away from me. I had to work hard, and overcome it all. I have gotten stronger from that experience. I know it takes a lot to come back from an injury."
>
> —*Candace Parker, Tennessee, 2007 NCAA Women's Basketball Champs*

Injuries can either break you or make you. One of the most depressing things an athlete can go through is suffering an injury. The pain of the injury does not even compare to the pain of watching from the sidelines. The way in which an athlete handles such adversity really determines how or if they come back. After you get over feeling sorry for yourself, you will eventually realize that you have to rehabilitate yourself in order to make a strong comeback. I know so many athletes who have had to overcome such tragedies. Some who were better after surgery, and some who were never the same. For some, the injury and time off made them hungry, and for some the discouragement and depression led them to self-doubt, fear of re-lapse, or loss of the their competitive edge. I talked to Serena Settlemier, National Pro Fastpitch Player for the Rockford Thunder, regarding her injuries. After the Doctors said she would never pitch again, she went on to win Conference player of the year at the University of Kansas. During the time where she was unable to pitch she worked harder on her hitting and smashed a record 22 homeruns in 2006. By the way, she still pitches. There are so many stories of athletes and non-athletes who have overcome tremendous obstacles. Their stories should motivate and inspire us to be the best that we can be and bring out that greatness that lies deep within us all.

I'M IN LOVE

No your not.

SHUT UP DAD! PARENTAL PRESSURE

Why do some parents even come to the games? Most of your kids don't even want you there. They would probably go 4-4 if you would just shut up (see Chapter 18). It is very difficult to be a parent and a coach. Here is an example. For a few months, I was privy to watch a MLB batting coach work with his son. His Son had/has so much talent, but perhaps lacked the focus to be consistent. Anyway, this kid would not listen to his father. I said to him one day, *"Yo, your father is a MLB batting coach, he is the batting coach for the world Champions, are you kidding me? You should try listening to him."* He still didn't listen to his father. So what makes you think your daughters and sons are really going to listen to you? It is a conflict of interest. You have to pay someone else to tell them the same thing you would have told them. That is the bottom line. So butt-out, sit back and enjoy the game—and get over it.

One of my most successful students, Maddy Coon, who was the NY State Gatorade player of the Year 2005. Certainly the most highly recruited HS softball player of her recruiting class. This is a girl who turned down UCLA. Who the hell turns down UCLA? Anyway, her father said something I thought was very profound. He said, *"The best thing I ever did for my daughter was stop coaching her."* You can stop reading this book right now, because that is it! I know some of you are not capable of doing that. The control probably defines you. He made that decision when she was about 12. The best thing you could do as a parent is to invest in a nice portable chair, with arms rests, and a cup holder, sit far away and keep quiet. That is if you have put your child in the right hands.

WHAT IF? FEAR OF FAILURE

The *Outcome Driven* athletes are the most inconsistent. I can tell who the outcome driven hitters are by the questions they ask me, or by their body language after a bad swing in practice. This type of hitter will show signs of frustration when they are having a bad day.

I believe that most people are not as afraid of failing as they are of being 'seen' failing. For example, when was the last time you got a high five for striking out? When was the last time your coach said nice job when you didn't get it done? So it is the judgment or response to our failing we get from our peers, parents, and coaches. These are the factors that make failing hard to deal with and what we fear most. It boils down to what we know our peers, parents, and coaches expect of us. But I always like my students to know what they expect of themselves. So after an 0-4 day, I will ask them the question, *"Did you hit the ball hard today?"* And if the response is YES, then we cannot be mad at that. The outcome driven players will be upset for making outs, when making outs, is obviously beyond their control.

Only immature athletes and crybabies throw equipment and tantrums when things don't go their way. A player must be taught how to fail. A little league player will think its okay to throw his bat, and doesn't realize that it is only a game. He thinks that the throwing of the bat will transfer the focus from the failure to the tantrum. Mature hitters understand the purpose and the necessity of failure. I watched my son, who is an excellent fielder, misplay a ground ball through his legs on a routine double play opportunity. He just stood there. The coach could not call time out and go and get him. He had to stand out there and endure the embarrassment. He knew he should have had it. But he needed to get the next one.

This spring, I am coaching an 11U travel baseball team. I told them in a loud and stern voice, that the consequences for crying are, *"You're off the team!"* Of course I am not going to throw an 11 year-old off the team. But I bet you I won't have any crybabies either. I also have a rule that I strictly enforce for batters and pitchers with regard to facial expressions and body language. We have enforced this with my 16U players since they were 12U. The rule is no one is allowed to look at an umpire: especially a hitter. And no pitcher is allowed to huff and puff or look up into the air with disbelief when calls don't go their way. If it happens, my players know that they just took put themselves on the bench.

UGLY or FAT PITCHER

I recently took a poll of about 15 or so HS level hitters, and I found this answer as a common distraction to come up twice. I found it funny at first, and then I realized that there are so many things that distract hitters and usually can be things we would never guess. Both hitters said, "They were distracted by an ugly or overweight pitcher." One hitter said, "it bothered her to see a pitcher's body fat sticking out of her uniform during the delivery." The other said she faced an ugly pitcher with a lot of facial hair and it made her laugh. This is real feedback from legitimate hitters with a lot of abilities. Wow!

COACHES COMMENTS: My Coach is a F@#$&%!

> *"Many men are slaves because one is an oppressor; let us hate the oppressor." Now, however, there is among an increasing few a tendency to reverse this judgment, and to say, "One man is an oppressor because many are slaves; let us despise the slaves."*
>
> —*The Thought-Factor in Achievement, Angelfire.com*

Yes. Most coaches are not very nice. Would you agree? Great, now that we have established that, can we play ball? I am so sick of these mental midgets using their psycho coaches as excuses for their own shortcomings. Get your mind on what you need to do and your coach's personality issues won't be such a big deal. If you just go out and bat .400 your coach won't seem so bad. I promise. Learn how to tune your coach down, and tune your objectives up. Make your coach background noise instead of the loudest thing you hear. If you are going to be an *emotional mess* every time your coach belittles you, then you have a long way to go. Mental abuse is what some would call it, but if you cannot handle it, then perhaps you should look to move to another program. But remember that everywhere you go, there will be some sort of adversity. There is no perfect situation. These Bobby Knight types of coaches are what makes us strong players and mentally tough. If you could play for these coaches, then you could play for anyone. There's always REC softball.

Respectfully avoid conversations with people (including your parents) who always have something negative to say about the coach. How can you focus on your coach's issues when you have your own issues to resolve? Start thinking about you and how you can contribute to the team's success and things will pan out. In most of these cases, the players are so concerned with how much the coach is an *A@#$%*, that they find themselves performing well below their abilities. Now you can blame the coach, or you can step up. Pick one. *BLAME THE COACH OR STEP UP!* Some body on your team is doing well in spite of the coach! Why not you?

Allow me to put a positive spin on crazy coaches. They are necessary. When an ordinary piece of carbon is pressed and tortured by the extreme heat applied to it, it eventually transforms into a diamond. That is you. Go through the fire, and come out as a diamond. Chances are you won't regret it. Use your deep hatred for your coach as a stepping stool toward success. Your coach's attitude should motivate you to SHOW THEM what you are really made of. But if you cannot find it in yourself to step up, then step out.

MY TEAM SUCKS

Why is there such a big difference in the level of competition at the HS level and the summer league or travel? The best advice I can give a person is GET OVER IT. It is what it is. I just received a text message from a player who is a senior in HS and already committed to a Division 1 program. The text message went something like this: "Oh God, I cannot take it, my team absolutely sucks!"

We cannot ignore the fact that HS baseball and softball are not always as competitive as your summer experience. Many HS programs aren't staffed with baseball or softball people. Also, the talent pool is not as vast as the summer travel team is. Therefore, it is not easy to stay motivated and maintain your high level of intensity. It is no secret that college recruiters don't even come to HS games. They are more interested in seeing you play against the best possible competition in order to get a true evaluation of your performance ability. In fact, HS statistics are not very valuable to coaches either, unless you hit like 20 homeruns. It is very difficult to know how strong your schedule is. I had a parent who was bragging about how his child's batting average was so much higher than another player's average. But his child was nowhere near as talented as the player with the lower batting average. The fact is, one played at a small school against even smaller schools and the other played against schools with 600-700 students in the senior class.

Below are some of the comments, observations, and complaints I often hear regarding HS vs. summer/travel:

- My coach knows nothing
- My outfield can't catch a fly ball
- The other players are not committed

- My team Sucks
- Our practices are so boring
- I feel like I am going backwards
- What if I quit?

I work with a lot of high-level HS players and almost none of them are very excited about their HS program. They feel that there are a lot of players who do not belong on the team and it is a waste of their time. This is something that every player has to deal with and it is not an excuse to perform poorly. In fact, it is an opportunity to excel and boost your confidence in order to stay in shape for the upcoming summer season. With the right attitude, your HS season will be a breeze, and over before you know it. With the right attitude, you can be a positive influence on your HS teammates and infect change. Instead of playing below your potential, you can inspire your teammates to play even better. With the wrong attitude, the HS season will seem like forever.

Some other common distractions could be moving fielders, fear of the curveball, team chatter/chanting, or a pitcher's grunt. So how do we get a player to be so focused that they would not even notice a low flying airplane? See the next Chapter 14, The Battle: Focus and Distraction.

14

Focus Phases: The Game Face

PIGEONS and EAGLES

This isn't about birds but really about focus. I call players who lack consistent focus, pigeons. Players who can focus consistently—They are more like Eagles. If you throw a piece of bread to the left of a pigeon he will chase it. If you throw another piece of bread to his right, he will abandon his pursuit of the bread on his right and chase the bread on the left. If you throw a stone, the pigeon will fly away and forget all about the bread altogether. Pigeons cannot focus past what is in front of them and are easily distracted. In fact, pigeons do not even have a concept of what they should focus on. How many athletes do you know to be pigeons?

Now Eagles on the other hand, are locked in to whatever their target is. An Eagle is extremely focused on their objective and cannot be sidetracked or distracted. If you throw a rock at an Eagle who is in pursuit, she will fly higher, maintain eye contact with her prey, and perhaps come back for it later. Now that's focus! Most players cannot rise above their obstacles. The Eagle type players always rise above their issues or distractions. Eagles are extremely clear about what they are focused on. How many athletes do you know to be Eagles?

Let's take a look at some of the common distractions of hitters and athletes in general. I am going to give you a sample of the thought process of an athlete with Pigeon Eyes. See if you can relate. *"Oh my God, I don't want to strike out again. Please don't throw me a curve ball. I hate curve balls. I wish my Dad would shut up—he never stops correcting me. This umpire sucks—that wasn't a strike. It was inside. Am I dropping my back shoulder? I can't believe he called that a strike. I don't want to make the last out."* In Chapter 13, we identified the CD's or Common Distractions.

You can see how the Pigeon Eyed player jumps from one thought to the next. Totally distracted and no control of his thoughts. Yes, I believe I just said CONTROL of THOUGHTS. This is very possible and so important. It must be practiced. When practiced, one can become very good at it. Good to the point where they can master the thoughts they entertain. And dump the thoughts they don't want to entertain. Do you manage your thoughts, or do your thoughts manage you?

FOCUS PHASES: The Game Face

GAMMA PHASE (Off-Field)

The Gamma Phase or Off-field focus is defined as whatever you do away from the field that would contribute to your on-field success. For example, weights, video analysis, eating properly, visualization, and proper rest. These are examples of off-field focus or the Gamma Phase. Some coaches go as far as to ban cell phone usage and fan/player interaction before and immediately after games. Certain dress codes when traveling or team meals before or after the game. Curfews, team activities and mental breaks such as bowling or movies are ways of perfecting the Gamma Phase of focus.

BETA PHASE (Pre/Post Game)

I call Pre and Post game focus the Beta Phase. An example of post game focus is going home after a game and writing in a daily journal. Write down the things you did that day, such as how practice went, how the game went, what pitcher you faced, pitch sequences, what pitch you hit, and what pitches she got you out on. This phase is a bit more intense than the Gamma Phase. The Beta Phase is also pre-game and could be the way in which you interact with teammates on the bus en route to the game. Perhaps you are by yourself listening to a particular song on your IPOD. Perhaps you are comfortable warming up with the same person. Maybe you are reading a book or watching your swing mechanics. Whatever you do, you have some sort of a game face. This doesn't mean you cannot engage others or laugh at a joke. It simply means you are getting mentally and emotionally prepared to play. This is so personal and individual. I have found that everyone is different. I know some who are extremely superstitious and others who will do small things like wear a rubber band on the wrist or eat a certain type of food before the game.

ALPHA PHASE (In-Game)

The Alpha Phase is our highest level of focus. There are three different levels of the Alpha Phase that we expect BIG TIME athletes to understand. There is level one, where the player is somewhat focused. There is also level two, where the player is more focused than level one. Then there is level three, where the player is the most focused. Unlike the Gamma and Beta Phases, the Alpha Phase of focus requires players to learn how to *'flip the switch.'* The switch is flipped from level one, to two, and then ultimately to three within the blink of an eye. Upon the flip of the switch, the right amount of mental energy is released. Different amounts of mental energy are required for different parts of play. For example, with one foot in the batter's box picking up the signs from the third-base coach, the player is at level one. When the hitter actually digs in and the pitcher is taking the sign from the catcher, the switch is flipped to level two. When the ball is actually in flight, the hitter flips the switch to level three, where the most intense level of focus is required.

Our actions should always line up with our mindset. Our thoughts don't always necessarily line up with what our body/actions does. There is typically a 5-9 second window between the batter digging in, the pitcher stepping onto the rubber, and the ball arriving at the contact point. It is during this 5-9 second window where we are in the Alpha Phase of focus. I say 5 to 9 seconds to compensate for baseball pitchers who are throwing from the stretch. If we are not in the Alpha Phase of focus here, then distractions become greater or more exaggerated. This is especially true for *pigeons or mental midgets*. It is the same for a fielder. A fielder should be in the Alpha Phase of focus and would be more relaxed in between pitches than he would be when the pitch is actually in flight.

An example of a player with a weak or under developed Alpha Phase will struggle most at level three. Think of all the hitters you know who struggle with slow pitching, but will rip fast pitching. Well these types of hitters struggle with maintaining level three long enough to wait for the incoming pitch. If it is a faster pitch, their wait time is short and they do not have to maintain level three. Hitters who are excellent Alpha Phase players, can wait on a junk ball pitcher and still crush if it were a power pitcher.

Sean O'Brien, a player who I have had the privilege of coaching and training is a red-shirt Junior at Virginia Tech and captain of the baseball team. Sean is currently batting .340, which is a big deal for any player who is facing ACC pitching. So I asked him what he does before the game.

> *"… mentally I will look to see if I have faced the starting pitcher before, and remember how he pitched me the last time. Based on this, I will come up with a game plan on how I am going to approach him. If I have not faced him before, I just think about a fastball approach until I see otherwise."*

10 Invisible Focus Killers

- Close game or lop-sided game
- Beginning or End of Game
- 1st game or second game of a DH
- Big Crowd or Small Crowd
- Fatigue or non-fatigue
- Dad watching or not
- How many hits do you already have
- Starting or Coming off the bench
- Playing my Favorite Position or Not
- Top or Bottom of the Order

15

Change My Mind: Seasonal Mind-Sets (3 Trimesters)

○ ○

"We are what we repeatedly do. Excellence then, is not an act, but a habit."

—*Aristotle*

PRACTICE STRATEGIES AND PERMANENT LEARNING

How to Develop Instincts consistent with the following:

Phase One (Off-Season):

- Assessment of Commitment Level
- Nutritional Element for Maximum Results
- Evaluate, Build and Maintain Strength, Flexibility, Speed, Agility, and overall Fitness
- Establish Clearly Defined Goals
- Intro/Review Basic Fundamentals
- Introduction/Review of Visual Routes and Mechanics
- 175-200 Quality Reps Daily

Phase Two (Pre-Season):

- Maintain Strength, Flexibility, Speed, Agility, and Overall Fitness.
- Perfecting of Rhythm and Timing

- Focus: Speed of the Game
- Discipline and Game Plan Development
- Recognition and Reaction: Secondary Pitches, Strikes and Balls, and In-Flight Adjustments
- 150-200 Quality Swings
- Drills: Tempo, Speed of the Game

Phase Three (In-Season):

- Time Management, Discipline and Focus
- Maintain Personal Strength and Fitness Needs
- Strong Legs and Fast Hands
- Being On-Time
- Review Basic Fundamentals
- Recognition and Reaction: Secondary Pitches, Strikes and Balls, and In-Flight Adjustments
- Address Specific Issues
- Tempo, Speed of the Game

OFF-SEASON (FALL/EARLY WINTER)

In the off-season there is a certain type of mindset that is necessary for proper development of movements in either swing or pitching/throwing. Off-season is a great time and the only time for really breaking down or tearing apart a hitter or pitcher. It also allows plenty of time to build them back up.

I am always amazed at how people think they can really improve during the third trimester, which is close to the beginning of the season or in-season. People call me all the time and ask me to work with their players like mid-season. In this situation, my first thought is, *"where were you in September, October, November, and December?"* The answer is probably playing a fall or winter sport. When one is in-season, it is virtually impossible to really learn and implement new concepts. Most hitters who do this probably never become comfortable with the new concept. They either spend more energy and focus on form/mechanics, or they eventually revert back to what is comfortable to them. Ultimately, they will lose much of their aggressiveness, which affects their confidence. This hitter only spirals down from there. It is so difficult for the mind to focus on being aggressive and confident, while worrying if form is correct.

PRE-SEASON (LATE WINTER)

Players with strong aptitudes can really get the most out of pre-season training. Here, we go from a slow tempo, to a more game-like speed or tempo. And to tell you the truth, I never like to slow up. I would rather maintain the game-like tempos, but each player is different. During this trimester of training, aptitude really means a lot. Hitters with low aptitudes will find themselves going backwards and as a coach, you'll be starting over every time you work with these hitters. In the pre-season phase, we should be focused on maintaining strength, game-like tempo, muscle memory and also implementation of stress as well. Some players look so good in the cage but cannot put it together in the game. Therefore, stress has to be added to the drills in order to match the stress of the game.

IN-SEASON (SPRING AND SUMMER)

I believe that what has been firmly planted cannot be uprooted. Training in-season is something that is very necessary in order to maintain what has been learned in the off-season and even during pre-season. It is important to continue to train, not only when things are going bad, but also when things are gong well. It is natural for a hitter to pick up habits or revert to old habits during the course of the season. Soft resets need to be performed in order to bring a hitter back to his default settings. This is sort of like having a computer problem, pressing control, alternate, and delete to reboot your computer and the issue goes away.

CHANGING STRENGTH LEVELS

After working with certain hitters all winter long and then sending them out to play in the spring, I notice that everyone has their own individual struggles. This is normal. However, I am finding that everyone does not make the necessary adjustments for success. Successful and consistent hitting is about making adjustments. You have to make adjustments from game to game, pitcher to pitcher, and from AB to AB, and sometimes pitch to pitch. Hitters who have the same approach all the time are bound to fail. Their very own frustration will take them right out.

A Brief Scenario:

Jennifer is 0 for her last 7. She hit 3 'atom balls' during these 7 AB's. Jen, is becoming frustrated and consequently concerned about her stats. It never occurred to her that she has hit a lot of hard hit balls right at the defenders. Anyway, she gets so emotional about her perceived slump that she begins to concern herself with mechanics and what she could be doing wrong. Her being over-analytical leads to a decrease in her aggressiveness. Next, her confidence is gone. Now Jen is in a place where most hitters never come back from. Self-Destruction begins …

Most great hitters never change their strength levels. They understand that the key to their success is their ability to control 2 things—(body) strength and (reaction) speed. How STRONG their legs are and how FAST their hands are. If those two things are not happening, a perfect swing won't help you. This is especially true of the in-season mindset for a consistent hitter.

I recently worked with 4 hitters who are currently half way through their High School season. Two of them are struggling and two are not. The two that are struggling came to me with weak swings, and the two who are not struggling came in with strong swings. Do you see my point? STRENGTH LEVELS are soooooo important.

I would say that about 85% of hitters that actually train, do not have the IN-GAME focus skills to take what they have learned in training onto the field. And if I may go a step further, most hitting instructors do not have the ability or the time to help them to make that transition. Most hitting instructors have a lot of technical knowledge, but it ends there.

It is easier to teach a player to have a great LOOKING swing than how to be successful on the field. That is the hard part of teaching. Theory vs. Reality. Just because it is in the book, doesn't mean it works for every hitter. Hitting and the teaching of it is so personal, individual, and sensitive. And I always ask the question to myself, *"Are you teaching this hitter to have a nice swing, or HOW TO HIT?"*

16

It's The Thought that Counts

✦

New swing or new brain

○ ○

"… I find myself working with hitters who really don't need a new swing as much as they do a new mindset …"

I was having a conversation with a highschool hitter the other day. She was bragging about how her school beat a specific pitcher. Here are her exact words, *"we beat Jessica 4-2 last season."* Now let me tell you why I have a problem with the way she worded this.

In baseball we say we beat a TEAM, not a person. We never give A PERSON so much credit. We don't make people so large or seemingly invincible. However, I've noticed that in softball, it is usually all about the pitcher. And pitchers are always so glorified. This is a mindset that lends to pitcher dominance. So as a hitter in softball, are you a hitter trying to get a hit or is she a pitcher trying to get you out? Read that question again: *so as a hitter in softball, are you a hitter trying to get a hit or is she a pitcher trying to get you out?*

Here is an alternative mindset. *"Last year we beat Triborough Highschool 7-3. They are gonna have problems getting me out this year. I can't wait to put it on 'em! Jessica is pretty good, but she better bring her A-Game. She had better hope I'm not on."*

INSIDE-OUT SWINGS

Should we teach hitters how to think like hitters? Of Course. Well, who is qualified to teach hitters how to think like hitters? Any good businessperson thinks like an entrepreneur. Every criminal thinks like a criminal. This poses the question, "Are hitters developed from the outside in or from the inside out?" I normally have an objective for my hitters when I am working with them. I have a goal for the 60 minutes of work we do and then I have a 4-6 month goal, and of course a 1-3 year goal. However, I am noticing that some people expect to be able to be consistent in just a few sessions.

Then some hitters have their own personal goals. They believe that if their swing looks better, then they will be better hitters. Here is what I know going into a session with a 14 or 15 year old player: If they can hit, I can help them, if they cannot hit then only God can help them. Hitting is learned more than it is taught. Hitting is learned more than it is taught. Hitting is learned more than it is taught.

I have a hitter who batted over .400 in college his freshman year. Then he went into a situation where he had transferred schools and his new coach wanted him to hit his way. This player has been my student since he was a little boy, and had never had any major changes in his approach. In the beginning it challenged him. I admit it also challenged me. Now he realizes that because he is a natural hitter, he can really hit anyway he has to.

THE MATRIX—WHAT IF a hitter could go into a store that sells customized swings? You could enter the store and purchase the perfect swing in one pill. Or what if you could purchase the following items in pill form: Attitude, Confidence, Focus, Relaxation, Concentration, Commitment, and Work Ethic—all in one pill? Now here is the catch: You can only buy one or the other—the perfect swing, or the perfect mindset. Which one would you purchase?

Let me help you. If you go for the perfect swing without the correct mindset, the perfect swing will always evade you. Your mind would be so jacked up; you would not be able to keep that *"perfect swing."* But if you go for the perfect mindset, you will always be able to achieve and maintain the "perfect swing."

As of late, I find myself working with hitters who really don't need a new swing as much as they do a new mindset. In fact, I have realized that if I change the swing without changing the mindset, my hitters will always be corrupted by their inability to manage their thought patterns.

It is sort of like giving someone a million dollars who is not very good at managing money. They'll be broke in 2 years or less. Well, if I give a hitter this *'knowledge of the elite'* and they are unable to manage it, it is almost safe to conclude they will be worse off than they started.

Therefore, we must begin to change the way hitters think. It is not always hitting mechanics that hinders maturity. In fact, it is rarely hitting mechanics. People always say it, *"It's in his brain, or it's all in her head."* How many people are training hitters how to think? Sports psychologists are very good at what they do and certainly serve their purpose, but are they really capable? Are they qualified to teach hitters or athletes how to think? I don't know, but I would be more comfortable listening to a sports psychologist who actually has competed at a high level in something besides Little League or academics.

GROW UP

I have heard some pretty good coaches tell hitters not to think or to simply, *"Stop thinking!"* Well, if you don't tell them what they should be thinking about, then what do you expect? It's like telling a child not to eat sweets, but you don't tell them what they should eat. Let's try an exercise:

Follow the steps below:

1. Take 20 seconds to clear your mind before reading step 2.

2. Do not think about a pink elephant.

3. I repeat, do not think about a pink elephant.

I can bet I know what you're thinking about. Do you see my point? This is why we teach in the positive. We never teach players what not to do. Instead, we teach them what to do! I often say that hitters have to grow up. The only way for hitters to actually GROW up is if the parents and coaches are nurturing them properly. When we think about hitters growing up, we see MATURE hitters and IMMATURE hitters.

ATTRIBUTES OF A MATURE HITTER

- Always has a Game Plan
- Swings at his pitch when ahead
- Lives for the next opportunity
- Extremely Self-Motivated
- Mostly On-Time (contact)
- Impeccable Work Ethic
- First and Last player at the field
- Great ATTITUDE even when he's not playing well
- TEAM first, me second

- Disciplined Diet
- Committed

ATTRIBUTES OF AN IMMATURE HITTER

- No Game Plan
- Swings at bad pitches when ahead
- Lives in the past
- Not very motivated
- Always late (contact)
- Bad Body Language when she is not doing well
- No Work Ethic
- Undisciplined Diet
- No Commitment

SUCCESSFUL TRANSITION TO THE FIELD

- Swing routines should be incorporated toward the end of BP
- Situational adjustments

Please understand that it is very difficult, probably impossible to have a GAME SWING that is identical to your PRACTICE SWING. It will never happen. My goal as a trainer is to get players to have their GAME SWING and their PRACTICE SWING appear to be as close as possible.

17

Reconciliation: Body and Mind Synchronized

o o o o o o o o o o o o o o o o o o o o o o o o o o o o o o o o o

"… We have an entire generation of hitters that are good but could be better. Perhaps they think too much. We have given them so much information and too many things to think about …"

LIVING IN THE PAST

Can you send your body into the past or future? Of course you can't. Can you send your mind into the past or future? Of course you can. Hitters do it all the time. Too many hitters are caught up into what has already happened or what is going to happen. Hitters thinking about that last AB or the low pitch the umpire called, or perhaps even the error they committed last inning. Another example of how athletes live in the past is past success. A homerun in the previous AB can sometimes be the worst thing that could happen. Players coming off a great season, sometimes refer back to that "great season" way too much. So it is all always about the now, the present, the here. Never about yesterday, last week, or last year, and certainly not so much about the outcome. Often times, we are not in control of the outcome. What we can control is the way we think! We can control what we think, and the body will always follow the mind or what we think.

The mind has to be in the present, which is the only place the body can be. If the mind is anywhere but the present, it is not in sync with the body. Modern day hitting coaches have done a great job in finding out all of this great information. However, we have done a poor job communicating it. Instead of producing great hitters, we have an entire generation of hitters that are good, but think too much. We have given them so much information and too many things to think about. And of course if you are thinking about your swing, you are thinking, not hitting. It is a classic case of PARALYSIS BY ANALYSIS. It can be very stressful for young hitters to concern themselves with so much technical knowledge. All this information we think we know, they don't need to know every intricate detail. I am just not convinced that hitters are hindered by physical swing mechanics to the extent that we coaches think. I have learned that hitters will never fully mature unless they learn to master the processes and patterns of thought.

WHAT THE HECK ARE YOU THINKING ABOUT?

Thoughts, feelings, perceptions, and emotions; this is thinking. There is a time to think, and a time not to think. When there is negative thinking these are distractions. We call it STINKIN' THINKIN.' Distractions disrupt focus and concentration. Focus and concentration are vital to success and consistency, especially in the clutch. Most hitters are what I call F.A.T. Fearful, Anxious, and Tense. They suffer from Fear (of failure), Anxiety, and Tension.
Fear (especially of failure):

- What if I disappoint my teammates?
- What if I disappoint my coaches?
- What if I don't play well?
- What if I get benched next game?
- What if I disappoint my parents?
- What if strike out?
- What if I walk a run in?
- What if I drop the ball?

Let us take a look at some of the sources of Anxiety:

- Worried about what my parents or coaches will think or say
- Worried about making mistakes
- I don't want to lose
- Worried about how good a pitcher is
- Concerned about form/mechanics
- Worried about called balls and strikes

This goes on at every level. Here is an email I received from a parent of 12 year-old.

Good Morning,

Will has learned some great skills under your guidance over the past few months. Will is the kind of kid that takes everything to heart. He is very afraid to do the wrong thing in a game. He feels that he has no margin for error. He is under the impression that one base running error or pitching error and he is finished.

He always strives to do his best, and his having a difficult time feeling that one mistake and he is in trouble. I have tried to explain to him that this is not the case, that this is a development league and that everyone makes errors. Could you spend a minute with him before the next game and let him know that all you expect is that he tries hard and that one mistake is not fatal.

Thanks

OVERCOMING TENSION (Tension and Muscle Tension)

TENSION is caused by fear of or stress due to failure. It is also caused by not meeting the expectations you have of yourself or others may have of you. This tension negatively affects your approach. Tension is increased when we inhale and hold it. When we exhale or breathe out, we release or decrease tension. This is why many athletes especially tennis players and softball pitchers will grunt. I am a big fan of the grunt for specific drills in order to make the body feel the release of tension at the time of contact or time to perform. Grunting ensures us of one thing—that we will exhale and the release of tension is sure to follow.

Coaches and parents who blurt out instructions during the game, coaches who give hitting lessons during the AB, I am indicting you. Let's be honest, most coaches are nothing more than good managers. They know how to put a line-up together, book umpires, make the phone calls for game changes and cancellations, find tournaments, book hotels, and manage a game. For all that labor, the reward is the opportunity to stand at 3B as "the coach." But are we really coaching? Are we really getting our players better?

The coaches who really get it, are the ones who bring in the appropriate people to help out with the things they know little or nothing about. Or they attend clinics and learn from others. No one person can know everything. In my profession it is sometimes a challenge for me to get even the most talented athletes better when working one on one. So I can only imagine how hard it must be for coaches to get an entire team of players better. Staying in the present is the key to keeping players focused on the process or in the moment. If you are not in the moment or staying in the present, then you are in the past or worried about what the future results will be.

STAY IN THE PRESENT

> *"You can't do anything about the past, but you can ruin a perfectly good present by thinking about it." "The past is history, the future is a mystery. Being alive in this moment is a gift. That is why they call it the present."*
>
> —*Zen Golf*

Hitters are *'slumping'* because they are either stuck in the past or dwelling in the future. Too many hitters are worried about past failures or what their batting average is going to be. They are focused on the outcome, and not the process.

FAILURE: WHAT IS IT REALLY! I heard someone say that failure is merely, success turned inside out. WHAT THE HECK IS A SLUMP? *Def. SLUMP: noun. 1. a noticeable decline in performance. 2. CG., A growth spurt.*

I just recently ran an advanced hitting camp for HS players. We discussed the concept of a slump. What is it exactly? I defined slump for them. I defined it as the inability to see your pitch and/or hit it hard. A slump is not failure. Nor is it prolonged failure. Many of them have gone from one level to another very quickly. And with this jump, they have experienced a jump in the level of pitching. It will be about a half a season of failure and learning before they mature into their new level. Even at the Division I level, most dominant softball pitchers are averaging 12 strikeouts per game.

Bridgette Quimpo, close friend and colleague, is someone who is far from a novice in Proper Player Development and Athlete's Emotional Counseling. She provides us with a perspective on slumps and what they really mean:

> *"Slumps, although more mental than physical, are merely the perception of the hitter and usually a response to past failures … reverting to the basics, positive visualization and thoughts, are great ways to break out."*

The Complete Game definition of Slump: A SLUMP IS A GROWTH SPURT. It is a necessary process, which allows real growth and maturity to occur. This is funny. People call me and say they're in a slump. Write this one down. **You cannot be in slump if you can't hit. If you cannot hit, this is the reason** *why you are not hitting. Only hitters who are at least pretty good, can be in a slump. Or hitters who have actually been hitting before.* Sorry about that, but its true. And if you have not put any real training time in, you have no right to be upset about your inability to hit consistently. Players: Stop crying and put some real work in!

Many people would say that Alex Rodriguez had a slump or a bad season in 2006. We have to admit that his season was a bit short of his usual domination of the league but a lot of players would love to have hit 35 HR's and drove in 121 RBI. So anyway, a man who refuses to live in the past and not allow statistics to define him has 12 HR's on April 21st. What is that? MLB history in the making. I would like to suggest to you that a slump is really a GROWTH SPURT. Yeah he won the MVP in 2005, had an off-season in 2006, but you better believe he has grown up now. After having experienced 2006 and what the fans and media put him through, he had some growth spurt. He will never repeat 2006 again. What A-ROD is doing in 2007 is something we will be seeing a lot of. It is funny how we sometimes have to go backwards to be propelled forward! The lessons we learn from our failure should thrust us forward. Whether good or bad, we are never stuck in the past.

Here is an example of someone who is stuck in the past: Joey is going into his 3rd AB. He is currently 2 for 2 and the first pitch he sees is way low. The umpire calls it a strike. Joey is upset about the call and his emotions are out of control. He is still thinking about the last strike called as the next pitch comes in. He swings wildly at a ball in the dirt, and quickly justifies his immature reaction by blaming the umpire. (blaming the umpire is something he learned from the immaturity of his parents in youth basketball and his coach in youth soccer). Of course Joey takes this entire AB into the next AB. An immature athlete will take this entire game into the next one.

Alternative: What would a mature hitter do? A mature hitter takes the bad call from the umpire and redirects his emotion to a positive thought—perhaps a deep breath. The pitch in the dirt that followed would have been a ball. So basically by learning how to 'turn the page,' a hitter can change an entire AB, Game, or even a Season.

Remember This: FOCUS on the PROCESS, not PAST FAILURES or FUTURE RESULTS. Most bad hitters are outcome driven and more focused on going 4 for 4 (the results) than the actual swing/process (the present). We need to focus on the present. The present is the ultimate gift, many of us take for granted. This is body and mind synchronization.

DIRECTING FOCUS and RIGHT THINKING

How can we help hitters to stay in the present moment? How can we get them to focus more on the process and less on the outcome? Is there a special way to train athletes in order to foster right thinking? There are drills that we use to develop the mind or the thought process of a hitter. We create challenges in practice that force the hitter to focus on a specific physical task within the process of the swing itself. By maintaining focus on a particular part of the process of the swing itself, other distractions are unconsciously ignored. This is something I call brainwashing. This is how we can cause distractions to become background noise rather than hindrances to perfect performance. Once hitters learn how to incorporate this type of thinking into their game, we are successful in producing what I call *right thinking*. Then, *right thinking* becomes merely a decision made by the athlete and has more to do with a player's attitude. Thus, attitude becomes a matter of choice—a decision. I will use myself as an example. Early in my baseball career, I had the attitude of a know-it-all, as do many male athletes. I was not very teachable when it came to hitting. However, once I developed the right attitude, one of humility, then I matured into a better hitter. I had to first make the decision to become teachable and humble myself under the tutelage of my mentors. From this example, we see how attitude is a decision. We actually brainwash athletes by teaching them how to think and respond in certain situations by re-creating game-like scenarios in practice.

Below is a quote from my mentor, Anthony Abbatine, who is the author of the internationally recognized Training Model for Frozen Ropes Training Centers, and has served as Special Advisor to Player Development for Mets, Redsox, Yankees, Astros, and Rockies.

> *"The brain can only effectively process one act or stimulus at a time (seeing the ball or thinking about seeing the ball compete for the brains attention). Creating clutter in training sessions will force the players to prioritize what is important in game sessions; players need to be aware when their brain switches over to the thinking/consciousness/past or future comparisons ..."*

18

The Psycho Dad: the Passive Parent

Def. <u>Psycho Dad</u>: pronunciation: 'sI-(")kO—'dad (noun) 1. A parent who goes to great lengths to provide an environment that ensures their child has all of the resources available to him/her for the best possible chances of success., Usually the father. 2. A term created by 'passive parents' to justify why they don't do what aggressive parents do. 3. An abusive, or perhaps pushy Dad who forces his child to be the best.

What has been firmly planted cannot be uprooted! Commitment and work ethic begins with someone pushing you in the right direction. Once pushed, once these things are instilled, they become apart of you. You will always live it and breath it. It is the only way. It comes from your parents!

Just like many people, I work out. I work out because I want to. My personality is such that I want to get the most out what I do. Therefore, I recently hired a trainer in order to "push" me. Mainly, because I want to be pushed, or to be honest, I need to be pushed. If I didn't have someone pushing me, I would not be able to bring the best out of myself. Let us not get the word *"push"* mixed up with the word *"force."* Should parents push their children?

> *"… the use of this terminology and other similar verbiage creates an inaccurate description of what responsibilities Parents have. This will potentially lead the parent down the wrong path … Parenting shouldn't change just because the involvement of a child is now athletic vs. academic, religious, musical, or whatever. The parent should provide a nurturing attitude and assist the child/athlete in experiencing each activity of interest."*
>
> *—Randy Coon*

Parental support is a big part of commitment, and commitment is everything when you talk about success. I have said this many times and it certainly rings true for so many of us. *"I have never met an elite player, who did not have a PSY-CHO DAD—NEVER!"* I was in the car picking up my son from HS baseball practice and he told me that he won the 2B job and his coach says he has the fastest hands at the position. I told my son that he should not be surprised because he has been trained properly. Not only has he been trained properly, he has been tortured and yelled at all his life in order for the excellence to be brought out of him. So naturally, he would stand out on a HS team full of players who lack commitment, work ethic, and talent. I told him not to get a bighead and continue to work hard.

Am I a Psycho Dad? I am not sure. I hope I am (that is def. no.1). But I will say that I have been very tough on my son regarding baseball and other life issues. Some people will get their children a tutor for every subject and have their kids locked in a room for days in preparation for schoolwork. And consequently, their children will excel in their schoolwork. Well, why do parents feel they are pushing, if they apply the same formula for sports. Professional instruction, personal trainer, nutritionist, SAT prep, competitive summer travel programs, tutor, piano lessons; what's the difference? You shouldn't be surprised when they suck if they have put little or nothing into it. You only get what you earn.

PSYCHO or STUPID

There are Psycho Dads and Stupid Dads. What's the difference? The line between the two is so fine. Here we go. Here is an example of a Stupid Dad: I had a conversation with my friend, who happens to be a HS Varsity softball coach. She was so upset. She said she just finished venting to her Athletic Director who would not support her in trying to get her parents under control. I never thought I would see the day when HS coaches have to really deal with parents (at least at this level). Why should they have to? I don't think my parents ever cared to speak to my HS coach about anything. She goes on to say that she has Dads that literally take off work to sit in on her practices and scrutinize everything she does. What is that? At what point do you cut the umbilical cord, get a life, and get over the fact that someone else besides you is in control now. Do these people have jobs? Of course she didn't have to tell me these guys were also summer coaches. These are Stupid Dads who are doing their daughters more harm than good.

I often hear people say that Dads like these are merely living their lives through their children. Have you ever heard that one? I have heard it a thousand times, but I do not agree with it. I think this might be the case some of the time. But parents these days do not want to be embarrassed on the field by their children. They enjoy the feeling of seeing their child succeed on the field so everyone can say *'your kid is awesome!'* So when their kid fails, it puts added pressure on the parent to push them harder and be over bearing tyrants. I think that is me too. I think I was like that also. But I believe I have grown up and become a better baseball parent. Now I sit out in center-field and do not say a word. I just enjoy watching my son do what he enjoys. And that is play the greatest game ever played. Sometimes.

A friend of mine assists me with my 16U baseball team. We have a great group of parents but they had to learn how to be great parents. So we had to teach them. Remember that parents, just like players, have to learn how to become better at it. As a coach, if you are not careful, your parents will be running you and your team. You have to set regulations and guidelines as to how your parents interact. This is important for your players, even at the youth level, for maximum in-game focus. How can players maintain a level of focus if their parents are hanging around the dugout and/or coaching from the stands?

19

Make it Happen: Goal Setting, Commitment, and Time Management.

After spending about an hour in a training session with a hitter, we had a brief conversation about what I recommended she do going forward. She told me she wanted to go to Arizona State University. I am a big believer in going for the gold, but when you set a high standard, your actions need to be in line with that goal. So my next question was how many times per week do you train? Do you see my point? A goal is only a goal if you are working towards it. If you are not working toward your goal, then it is only a dream.

The fact that we should set goals should really go without saying. Goals need to be set and many athletes shy away from this because they are afraid of failing. All goals should be realistic, specific, and measurable. Goals should be something that constantly reminds you of why you exist. You can hang up pictures and small cut outs around your room or on the refrigerator to serve as small reminders.

After you establish your goals, it is vital that you devise a strategy for attaining what you have written. This requires discipline, parental support, and of course commitment. I have found that many people do not understand the true definition of commitment. I coach a 16U College Showcase baseball team and the definition of commitment is posted on our website. And believe it or not, many of them still don't get it. Commitment is something only parents can teach their children-not the coach. If the parents are constantly pulling them out of their commitments, it teaches the child that commitment means nothing. I actually had parents of players at the youth level, come to me and say, *"We are committed but we can't make it this weekend,"* or *"we are committed, and we will be there when we can make it."* And what is crazy is that they see nothing wrong with these statements.

Athletes and people in general, who lack Time Management skills will find themselves rushing through life, cramming, and never getting anything done. This creates anxiety, and it is difficulty to perform under this type of stress. For example, the starting pitcher who arrives at the park thirty minutes before game time is sure to fail. Or if our term paper is due tomorrow and you have just begun typing it, when you knew about it two months ago, you will be fatigued at the 10am double-header in the morning.

I have outlined some of the many things successful people know and do.

- Successful people understand that Time Management is Life Management.

- Successful people can see themselves where they want to be.

- Successful people know how to act the part, even when they aren't (yet).

- Successful people are very good at modeling themselves after people who are where they would like to be, for success.

- Successful people learn how to like themselves.

Athlete Goal Setting Worksheet

S.M.A.R.T. GOALS

Whether athletic or academic, the most effective goals are designed to be S.M.A.R.T.

Specific, Measurable, Attainable, Realistic, Tangible with a target date

---

Goals must be:

    a.   important to you, personally

    b.   within your power to make happen through your own actions

    c.   something you have a reasonable chance of achieving

    d.   clearly defined and have a specific plan of action

Outcome Goals—Outcome goals are set based on results such as winning a game or getting a hit. These types of goals are not recommended because they are based on not only your ability and efforts but the ability and efforts of your opponent as well. Basically, you are not in control of the outcome. For example, you may pitch the game of your life but lose on an error in the extra innings. Or you may hit four line drives, but right at the defenders. Therefore, going 4-4 or winning the game would be outcome goals. I do not recommend outcome goals.

GOAL SETTING EXERCISE:

    1.   Write down your goals/objectives next to the roman numerals below.

2.   Write down the necessary steps to achieve your goal or objective next to the letters.

My (long-range) goals to complete in the next 2-3 years are:

I.

    a.

    b.

    c.

II.

    a.

    b.

    c.

III.

    a.

    b.

    c.

My (mid-range) goals to complete in the next 1 year are:

I.

    a.

    b.

    c.

II.

    a.

    b.

    c.

III.

    a.

b.

c.

My (short-range) goals to complete in the next 4-6 months are:

I.

a.

b.

c.

II.

a.

b.

c.

III.

a.

b.

c.

My (immediate) goals for the 30 days are:

I.

a.

b.

c.

II.

a.

b.

c.

III.

    a.

    b.

    c.

_____

EVALUATE YOUR TIME MANAGEMENT:

How much time have you set aside to meet your goals (above)?
Does your time allocation reflect the priority of your goals?
Can your uncommitted hours be reallocated to meet your priorities?

How committed are you? Here are the top excuses for not training or practicing for baseball or softball and a scale of 1-5 to describe your attitude for each excuse over the past month. Be honest:

1=Not at all
2=Sometimes
3=Moderately often
4=Often
5=All the time

FREQUENCY	REASON
	I'm Too tired
	I'm Too busy
	I have more important things to do
	I'll do it tomorrow
	I don't need to workout/train
	I want a day off
	No big deal if I miss one day
	I'm just not feeling motivated today
	I just don't feel like training

I need to just recuperate

(add for total)

Score: _____ 10-14=committed, 15 or higher=non-committed

Website: www.complete-game.net
Email: info@complete-game.net

85612465R00055

Made in the USA
Lexington, KY
02 April 2018